Kunsthistorisches Museum

History, Architecture, Decoration

kunst
historisches khm
museum

Cäcilia Bischoff

Kunsthistorisches Museum

History
Architecture
Decoration

Published by
Sabine Haag

Christian Brandstätter Verlag

Owner and Publisher:
General Director
Dr. Sabine Haag
Kunsthistorisches Museum
Burgring 5
1010 Vienna

Text and Concept:
Cäcilia Bischoff

Editor:
Elisabeth Herrmann

Translations:
Joshua Stein

Art Director:
Stefan Zeisler

Photographic Direction:
Stefan Zeisler

Photos:
Andreas Uldrich
Alexander Rosoli
Arnold Pöschl
Silvia Wimmer
Elisabeth Kudlicky
Hanna Christoph
Stefan Zeisler
Cäcilia Bischoff
Wilfried Seipel

Unless otherwise indicated: © KHM

Picture editing:
Sabine Sommer

Layout:
Peter Knehtl
Marc Jina

Printing and Binding:
Grasl Druck und Neue Medien, Bad Vöslau

Short Title:
C. Bischoff
Kunsthistorisches Museum
Vienna, 2010

ISBN 978-3-85497-187-0
All rights reserved.

© 2010 Kunsthistorisches Museum, Vienna
© 2010 Christian Brandstätter Verlag, Vienna

German National Library bibliographic information:
The German National Library lists this publication in the
German National Bibliography; detailed bibliographic
information is available on the Internet at http://dnb.d-nb.de.

1st edition

Christian Brandstätter Verlag
GmbH & Co KG
1080 Vienna, Wickenburggasse 26
Austria
Telephone (+43–1) 512 15 43–0
Fax (+43–1) 512 15 43–231
Email: info@cbv.at
www.cbv.at

Staircase with Canova's *Theseus and the Centaur* and ceiling painting by Mihály Munkácsy.

Contents

1891 – The Museum Completed

Vestibule. Decorated marble floor and stairway leading to Egyptian and Near-Eastern Collection.

Foreword

Very soon after publication two years ago of this magnificent volume on the history, architecture and decoration of Kunsthistorisches Museum – an initiative of my predecessor as General Director, Wilfried Seipel – the wish for an edition in English was expressed. I am very pleased indeed that we have been able to fulfil this wish in a relatively short space of time, and present to the English-speaking public an authoritative work documenting this "*Gesamtkunstwerk* of Historicism", as the museum has been dubbed.

The museum on Vienna's Burgring has been home to the collections of the former ruling dynasty since 1891 and every year attracts culturally interested guests from around the world. Visitors experience the "Ringstrasse" style in all its sumptuousness as soon as they enter the vestibule. No expense was spared in the use of materials in order to create an ambience worthy of the imperial art collections. Throughout the museum the decoration of the interior reflects the objects exhibited. The foremost artists of the Ringstrasse Era all had a hand in the museum's decoration. The magnificent cupola hall, which is adorned with effigies of the most important art patrons of the House of Habsburg and can be characterised as a temple dedicated to the dynasty's fame, never fails to impress visitors.

Since publication of the German-language edition of the book an important development has taken place: the ministry responsible for Austria's cultural heritage has appropriated the funds necessary to permit renovation of the Kunstkammer galleries, which have been closed to the public since 2002. The reopening of this major area of the collections of Kunsthistorisches Museum is now planned for late 2012.

Cäcilia Bischoff's achievement as author of this work is exemplary: she had painstakingly documented the fascinating story of the museum's construction, bringing to light new archival sources, historic plans and photographs, as well as describing in hitherto unprecedented detail the decorative programme of the museum's façades and interiors. Stefan Zeisler and the museum's photography studio have produced splendidly evocative pictures to illustrate and complement the text; they deserve my particular thanks. Joshua M. Stein succeeded in producing under a tight deadline the English text, which faithfully and sensitively reproduces the original. I would like to express my appreciation too to the director of our Publications Department, Elisabeth Herrmann, for overseeing the publication of the volume. I am also grateful to Christian Brandstätter Verlag for its readiness to publish an English-language version of the work. The establishment of the International Friends of KHM in New York in September 2010 represents another important step toward making our museum better known in the English-speaking world; I am confident that this lavishly illustrated and carefully researched tome will contribute greatly to the same end.

Sabine Haag
General Director, Kunsthistorisches Museum

View from vestibule
towards entrance to
Kunstkammer

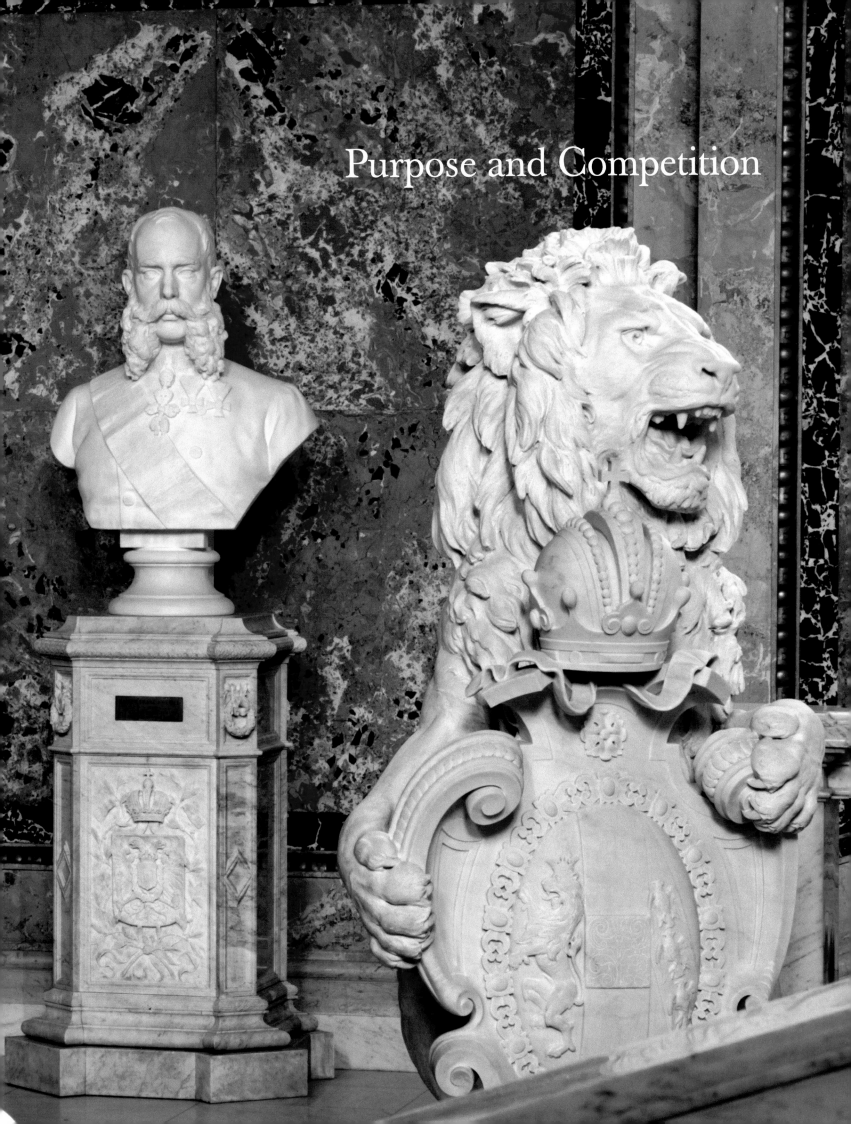

Purpose and Competition

Previous double page: Staircase, in the foreground statues of lions holding coat of arms (Edmund Hofmann von Aspernburg), in the background marble bust of Emperor Franz Josef I (1873, Kaspar Zumbusch).

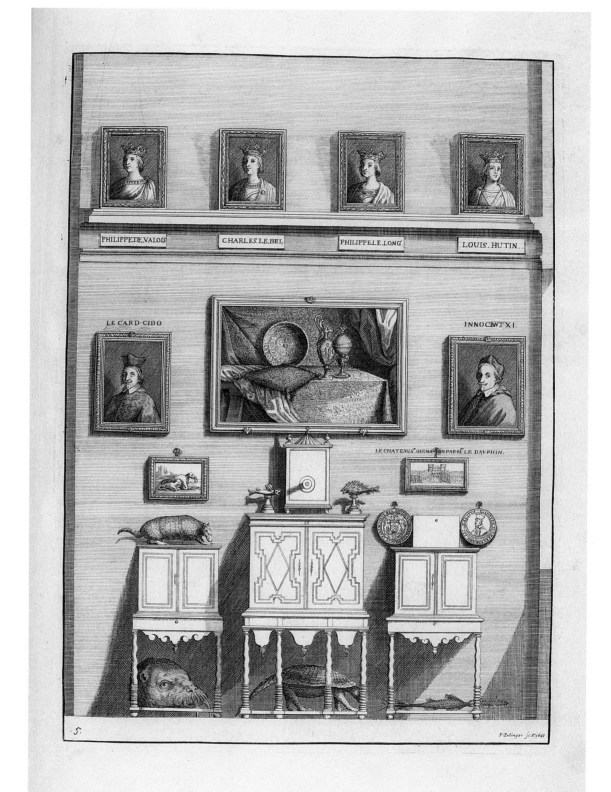

"Le Cabinet de la Bibliothèque de Sainte Geneviève" from Claude Du Molinet, *Divisé en deux parties,* Paris (Dezallier), 1692. Vienna, Kunsthistorisches Museum, Library, 1.180.

The Task.
A Brief Historical Retrospective

The construction of the *mouseion* of ancient Alexandria was certainly one of the most prominent milestones in the long development of the modern museum. This research institution was established in 248 B.C. under Ptolemy I Soter, one of the successors to Alexander the Great. The most famous part of the institution, which was dedicated to the muses, was without doubt its library. Astronomical, mathematical, botanical, and zoological studies were also pursued, and corresponding collections assembled. At the same time in Hellenistic Rome there developed private collections – to a large extent based on Greek war booty – which encompassed pearls and gemstones, silver plate and textiles, vases, paintings and sculptures. The fashion was indeed so widespread that Vitruvius in his architectural treatise included a floor-plan for a house with a special room for collections.

The Greek word *mouseion* (Latin: *museum*) originally denoted sacred precincts dedicated to the muses of the sciences and arts. Altars, and less frequently temples, were constructed on mountain peaks, in groves and grottos. The sacred precincts became known as places of instruction and study, and also offered a suitable location for literary competitions. Indeed, the need to remove certain objects from the circuit of economic activities is documented persuasively by the tombs of Egypt and China, to cite but two early examples.[1] Words such as 'bibliothek', 'pinakothek', 'glyptothek', were later adopted from the Ancient World. Knowledge of the existence and structure of these institutions was never lost entirely. Only in the later Middle Ages was the tradition revived based first on ecclesiastical treasuries, followed by cabinets of curiosities and early art collections. Bramante's statuary courtyard in the Belvedere of the Vatican (1503–10) long remained unique however. It was only in the second half of the sixteenth century that art collections and cabinets of wonders at the courts of western and central Europe and the sculpture collections of the Medici, laid the foundation for the subsequent development of modern museums in the second half of the eighteenth and early nineteenth centuries.[2] Among the early collectors, founders, and builders were Archduke Ferdinand

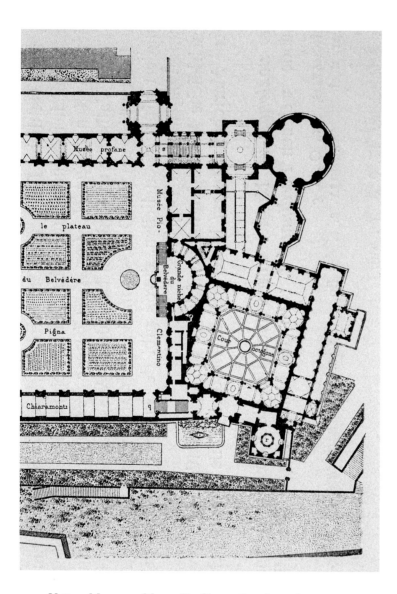

Vatican Museums, Museo Pio Clementino, floor plan
(detail). Heinrich Wagner, *Handbuch der Architektur,* part 4,
vol. 6, fascicle 4: Josef Durm, Hermann Ende (eds.), *Gebäude
für Sammlungen und Ausstellungen,* 2nd ed., Stuttgart, 1906,
ill. 343.

of Tyrol (Ambras Castle), Emperor Rudolf II, the
Saxon electors in Dresden, the dukes of Bavaria in
Munich, and in Italy, Lorenzo de' Medici and Pope
Julius II. At first, princely collections were housed in
existing or newly constructed palaces and accessible
only to a select public. Collections of ancient sculpture, paintings, libraries with cabinets of engravings
and coins, musical instruments, assemblages of art
and curiosities – all of these are reflected in diverse
architectural plans. In addition, picture galleries and
private art cabinets belonging to the middle classes
arose, in particular in the northern and southern
Low Countries.

The first buildings constructed independently of a
princely residence and solely for the purpose of
housing an art collection were the Villa Albani in
Rome (1746 ff.; architect: Carlo Marchionni, advisor:
Johann Joachim Winckelmann) and the Museum
Fredericanum in Kassel (1769–79; architect: Simon
Louis du Ry). In the Museo Pio Clementino in the
Vatican in Rome (1773 ff.; architects: Gaetano
Marini, Michelangelo Simonetti, Giuseppe Campo-
rese) changes were made to an existing structure.
The building's ceremonial staircase, grand entrance
hall, and cupola hall, where highlights of the collection were displayed, as well as differentiated types of
exhibition galleries were to become a model for
purpose-built museums. At the end of the eighteenth
century, the great French architects devoted their
attention to designing museums, with ideal plans
being published and academic prizes awarded.
Contemporaneous with developments in France, and
as a consequence of the centralisation of royal art
collections, especially in Vienna and Berlin, new
requirements and needs began to take shape. Extensive art collections were reorganised and classified,
and an approach to arranging and hanging artworks
developed that was based on scholarly considera-

tions. The Habsburg Kaiserlich Königliche Bilder Gallerie (Imperial Royal Picture Gallery) was initiated by Empress Maria Theresia in 1776. Under the directorship of Christian von Mechel, the gallery was moved from the Stallburg, one of the oldest sections of the Hofburg or Imperial Palace, in Vienna, to the Upper Belvedere palace, and opened, more or less, to the public. With the French Revolution it became politically possible to permit access to formerly princely collections. From 1793 a broad section of the public was allowed to view the former royal art collections on display at the Muséum Français (after 1796: Musée Central des Arts). The museum established scholarly and administrative services, produced catalogues, and labelled the works. The methods and solutions developed were adopted as an example all over Europe. The architects Charles Percier and Pierre-François-Léonard Fontaine provided the halls of the Grande Galerie with skylights during the years 1805–10. This technical innovation was to prove trendsetting, and by 1836 had become a standard feature in Klenze's Pinakothek in Munich. An essential work for

Drawing of a gallery wall in the Stallburg, 1733; gouache on parchment. Among the paintings depicted are Francesco Solimena's *Presentation of the inventory of the Stallburg to Karl VI by Gundacker Graf Althann, Imperial Director of Construction*, 1728 (KHM, Picture Gallery, Inv. No. 1601). From: Ferdinand Storffer, *Bildinventar der kaiserlichen Sammlung in Wien*, 3 vols., 1720, 1730, 1733, KHM, Gemäldegalerie.

any academically trained architect was Jean Nicholas-Louis Durand's *Précis des leçons d'architecture* (1802–05). The *Précis* included floor-plans, views and cross-sections that could be employed in a modular fashion for building projects of all kinds, among which museums already numbered. Thus in the early nineteenth century both those commissioning buildings and architects had models which were considered prescriptive: for façades and interiors, a decorative idiom that harked back to antiquity; arrangement of the structural elements around the building's centre (frequently a rotunda), and a combination of large galleries with smaller adjacent cabinets. The museum had by now evolved into a place of learning and bearer of national identity. It also became detached from palace architecture and developed into an autonomous genre. In 1800, Karl Friedrich Schinkel, who had been schooled in the French tradition, published his plan for a model museum embedded in an antique landscape, which however was never to be realised. Ambitious building plans of German princes were carried out only after Napoleon's final defeat, at first in Munich and Berlin. Leo von Klenze's Glyptothek on a newly created square in Munich (1816–30) and Schinkel's Altes Museum constructed opposite the palace of Prussia's kings in Berlin (1822/25–30) herald the beginning of a long series of projects. With his

Berlin, Altes Museum. Floor plan of the upper level showing original scheme for hanging paintings. Gustav Friedrich Waagen, *Verzeichniß der Gemälde-Sammlung des Königlichen Museums zu Berlin,* Berlin, 1833.

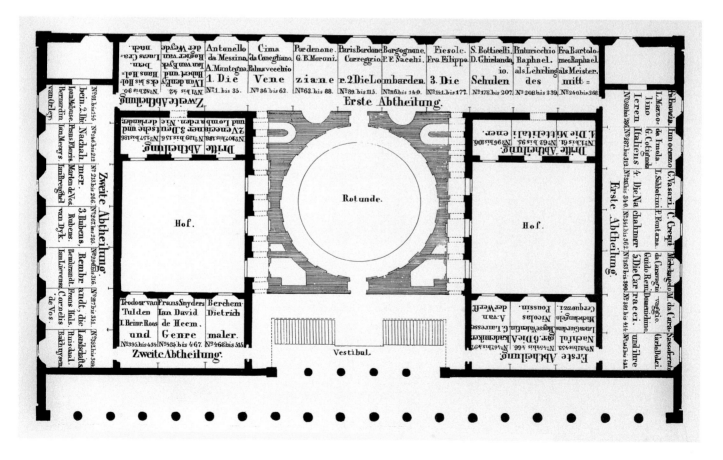

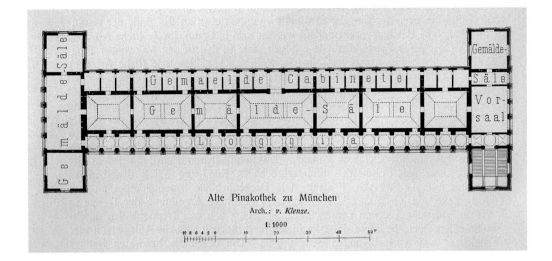

Munich, Alte Pinakothek, floor plan. Heinrich Wagner, *Handbuch der Architektur,* part 4, vol. 6, fascicle 4: Josef Durm, Hermann Ende (eds.), *Gebäude für Sammlungen und Ausstellungen,* 2nd ed., Stuttgart, 1906, ill. 374.

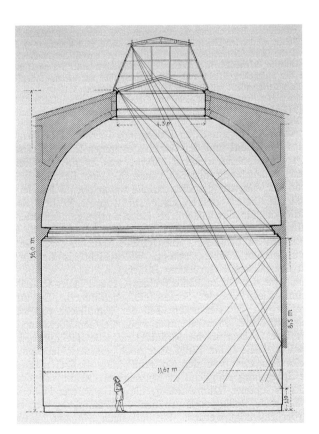

Munich, Alte Pinakothek, Cross section of a hall in the picture gallery. Heinrich Wagner, *Handbuch der Architektur,* part 4, vol. 6, fascicle 4: Josef Durm, Hermann Ende (eds.), *Gebäude für Sammlungen und Ausstellungen,* 2nd ed., Stuttgart, 1906, ill. 411.

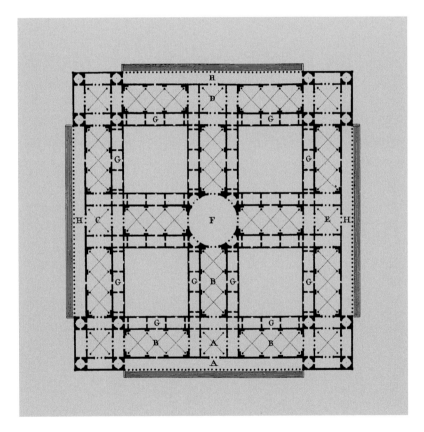

Jean Nicolas Durand, design for a museum after *Précis des leçons d'architecture,* 2nd ed., Paris, 1817.

museum Schinkel created an enduring model. It was based on two courtyards separated only by a central cupola area with staircase, and had a series of galleries that permitted works of art to be displayed interchangeably.

It had become a matter of course not to leave concepts for galleries and hanging pictures to architects alone. Klenze corresponded with Goethe and Schelling, while in Berlin, Alois Hirt, Wilhelm von Humboldt and Carl Friedrich von Rumohr acted as consultants. The creation of sculptural decoration was delegated to prominent sculptors, whilst the painting of the interior was among the major commissions of the period. In planning the Munich Pinakothek, which was constructed on a newly created square, Klenze first conducted an inventory of the picture collection, classified the works chronologically, and only then calculated the required number of rooms.

Munich, Alte Pinakothek, southern façade. Photograph, 1926. Munich, Bayerische Staatsgemäldesammlung, Inv. No. 26/598 (© Alte Pinakothek).

Munich, Alte Pinakothek, Rubenssaal. Photograph, 1926. Munich, Bayerische Staatsgemäldesammlung, Inv. No. 26/589 (© Alte Pinakothek).

Gottfried Semper, picture gallery viewed from courtyard of the Zwinger as it appeared in 1894. Dresden, Landesamt für Denkmalpflege Sachsen (© Landesamt für Denkmalpflege Sachsen).

Gottfried Semper, Gemäldegalerie Dresden, vestibule following restoration of painting by Carl Gottlieb Rolle, 1993. Dresden, Landesamt für Denkmalpflege Sachsen (© Landesamt für Denkmalpflege Sachsen).

Theater und Sehenswürdigkeiten.

K. K. Hofburg-Theater.

Die Maler.

Lustspiel in 3 Aufzügen von Ad. Wilbrandt.

Personen.

Oswald, Maler . . . . . Hr. Sonnenthal.
Werner, } Maler, ... Hr. Förster.
Simion, } Oswald's . . . Hr. Baumeister.
Modest, genannt } Freunde
Plato,
Sandberg, Banquier . . . Hr. Mitterwurzer.
Blume . . . . Hr. Schöne.
Frau von Willnig . . . . Fr. Negro.
Leonore von Seefeld, deren
Tochter, Wittwe . . . . Fr. Gabillon.
Else, Werner's Schwester . Frl. Baudius
Pauline, } Plato's Cousinen Frl. Antonie Link.
Ulrike, } . . . . Frl. Hauenthal.
Müller, genannt Ubique, Haus-
meister der Maler . . . Hr. Arnsburg.
Gerichtsvollzieher . . . . Hr. Ferrari.
Gendarm . . . . Hr. Jehly.
Anton, Farbenreiber . . . Hr. Köhler.
Die neue Decoration, ein Maler-Atelier darstel-
lend, von Hermann Burkhardt, Decora-
tionsmaler des k. k. Hofburg-Theaters.

Anfang 7 Uhr.

K. K. pr. Theater an der Wien.

Isak Stern,

einer von unsere Leut'.

Posse mit Gesang und Tanz in 3 Akten und
8 Bildern von O. F. Berg.

Anfang 7 Uhr.

K. K. pr. Theater i. d. Josefstadt.

Zum ersten Male:

Die Lieder des Musikanten.

Volksstück mit Gesang in drei Abtheilungen
(fünf Aufzügen) von Rudolf Kneisel.
Musik von Ferdinand Gumbert.

Anfang 7 Uhr.

K. K. Hof-Operntheater.

170. Vorstellung im Jahres-Abonnement.

FANTASCA.

Großes Zauber-Ballet in 4 Akten nebst einem
Vorspiel (zwölf Bilder) von Paul Taglioni.
Musik von Hertel.

Personen.

Don Rodrigo de Merino, spa-
nischer Grand . . . . . Hr. Massini.
Fantasca, seine Tochter . . Frl. Salvioni.
Die Duenna . . . . . . Frl. Basseg.
Floramour, provençalischer
Edler . . . . Hr. Frappart.
Espéron, sein Stallmeister . Hr. Price.
Ritter aus verschiedenen Län-
dern, um Fantasca freiend } Hr. L. Frappart.
} Hr. Couqui.
Romero, ein Hidalgo, Flor de
las Espadas genannt . . . Hr. Haßreiter.
mächtiger Zauberer . . . Hr. Beau.
Aglaia, seine Favorite . . Fr. Telle.
Scroll, Genius des Lichts . Frl. Mauthner.
Eine Wassernymphe . . . Frl. Wilschack.
Ein Rechwind . . . . . Frl. Richpini.
Gnomus . . . . Hr. Spartian.
Ein Küchenmeister . . . . Hr. Spartian.
Eine Möhrin . . . . . . Frl. Charles.
Die Fee Aquaria . . . . Frl. Petermann.
Don Rodrigo's Hofstaat: Ober-Ceremonienmei-
ster, Hofherren und Hofdamen, Pagen Ritter,
Stallmeister, Hellebardier ꝛc.
Melchasschef's Hofstaat: Die Großen des Hofes,
Ehrendamen, Priester Ahriman's, Favorit-
Sclavinnen, Bajaderen, Almeen, Amazonen,
Siamesen, Tänzer, Gaukler, Sklaven beiderlei
Geschlechts, Mohren, Zwerge ꝛc.
Aquaria's Hof: Najaden, Undinen und Wasser-
geister.
Pygmäen. Zwielten. Phantastische Erscheinungen.
Rechwinde, Sturmwinde ꝛc. Volk. Zigeuner.

Vorspiel: 1. Bild: La Bonne-aventure.
I. Akt: 3. Bild: 1) Cortège des Prétendants,
2) Divertissement espagnol.
II. Akt: 4. Bild: L'Epreuve (Pas d'action).
— Ballabile: Papillons, Guêpes, Mouches,

Lucioles etc. etc. — 6. Bild: La Negresse.
— Polka: Rats et serviteurs galants.
III. Akt: 7. Bild: Les Esquimaux. — Les
Folles-brises. — La Tempête (Borcas,
Nord, Süd und Aeolus). — 8. Bild: Pas
d'action. — Ballabile, Guerrières de l'Ile
Idalia.
IV. Akt: 9. Bild: Grande marche et fête in-
diennes. — 10. Bild: Danse: Fleurs des
champs avec Floramour et Espéron méta-
morphosés. — 12. Bild: Apothéose.
Die neuen Decorationen sind von den k. k. Hof-
theatermalern Herren Karl Brioschi und Her-
mann Burghart.
Neue Kostüme nach Zeichnungen des Historien-
malers Herrn Franz Gaul.
Maschinerien vom k. k. Maschinen-Inspektor Herrn
G. Drellich.

Strampfer-Theater.

(Stadt, Tuchlauben 16.)

In der Mark.

Schauspiel in 5 Akten von Hans Hopfen.

K. K. priv. Carl-Theater.

Ein Ehepaar aus dem Volke.

Pariser Genrebild in 1 Akt von Lambert
Thiboust, deutsch von Julius Hopp.

Der Bojar,

oder:

Wie denken Sie über Rumänien?

Lustspiel in 1 Akt von Gustav v. Moser.

Eine Vereinsschwester.

Schwank mit Gesang in 1 Akt, nach einem Stoffe
von B. Mannstädt von Anton Langer.
Musik von J. Brandl.

Sehenswürdigkeiten.

Donnerstag.
Stephanskirche, Besteigung des Thurmes am
Besten um 3 Uhr Nachmittags.

Bibliothek und Kupferstichsammlung des Erzher-
zogs Albrecht, Augustinerbastei. Von 9—1 Uhr.
Naturaliencabinet von 9—1 Uhr.
Oesterreichische Kunstindustrie-Ausstellung im
k. k. Oesterr. Museum am Stubenring, von
10—3 Uhr.
Gemäldegalerie des Grafen Czernin, Josefstadt,
Paradeplatz 9. Von 10—2 Uhr.
Münz- und Antikencabinet von 10—2 Uhr.
Anstalt für erwachsene Blinde, Josefstädter-
straße 62, von 9—5 Uhr.
Artillerie-Arsenal-Museum, k. k., außer der St.
Marxer Linie, von 9—3 Uhr. Eintrittskarten
bei der Arsenaldirection.

Alle Tage zu besichtigen.

Theseus-Tempel im Volksgarten.
Augustiner-Hofpfarrkirche mit den Grabmälern
der Erzherzogin Christine und des F. M. Daun.
Josephs-Akademie (pathologisches Museum), Alser-
grund, Währingergasse, von 11—1 Uhr.
Zeughaus, am Hof 10. Von 9—12 und von
3—6 Uhr.
Hofbibliothek, Josefsplatz, von 9—4 Uhr.
Hof-Jagd- und Sattelkammer und Hofmarstall
außer dem Burgthor.
Fürst Liechtenstein's Gemäldegalerie, Alsergrund,
Porzellangasse 33. Von 9—12 und 3—6 Uhr.
Krafft's Schlachtgemälde im Invalidenhause,
Landstraße, Hauptstraße.
Dessort's Museum: Am Schottenthor,
Franzensring 22, neben Café Hembsch. Per-
manente Ausstellung, anatomisches Museum
in 2 Abtheilungen, mit neuen Modellen.
Glasphotographien, 2500 Ansichten. — Paris
zur Zeit der Commune, die Ruinen und Bar-
rikaden in 200 Darstellungen. — Eröffnet
täglich von 8 Uhr Früh bis 7 Uhr Abends. —
Dienstag und Freitag Nachmittags von 2 Uhr
ab 7 Uhr Abends nur für Damen.

Firgisser's Salon, Rudolfsheim,
Grenzgasse, vis-à-vis dem Hotel Schwender:
Naturgetreue mechanisch-plastische Darstellung
einer steierischen Hochalpenpartie und der Sem-
meringbahn. Zu besichtigen jeden Donnerstag Nachmittags von 3 bis 6 Uhr.

Lotto-Ziehungen: Am 29. November 1871.
Prag 55 80 89 72 24 | Lemberg 5 23 1 42 4
Trient 21 16 53 54 77 |

Hierzu ein halber und ein Viertelbogen Anzeigeblatt.

The month construction commenced, *Wiener Zeitung*, 30. 11. 1871, Vienna, Österreichische National-bibliothek, Picture Archive (© Österreichische Nationalbibliothek).

On the Eve of Construction.
The Origins of the Ringstrasse

The origins of Vienna's Ringstrasse date to the reign of Maria Theresia.[3] As early as 1770 the Imperial Court questioned the defensive utility of the ring of fortifications around Vienna. The construction of the city walls had started around 1200 and been extended under the Babenberg duke Leopold V, during whose rule the Baroque line of fortifications was also built. Eventually, however, only the glacis – an area around the city up to 450 metres wide established in 1663 – in which construction was prohibited for strategic reasons, was levelled: a road for vehicles was laid out around the city as were pedestrian paths joining the city with its suburbs. The "Bastey" became a favourite place for strolling, especially because "one was safe from horses and wagons, free of dust, and had a lovely view of the suburbs and nearby scenery". The "Burg Bastey" in particular, which had been planted with trees starting in 1798, attracted strollers: huts and other small buildings were erected despite the ban on construction. The summer premises of a café were open every evening, and the entire square illuminated and filled by "hundreds of chairs", allowing visitors to enjoy "fine music played on wind-instruments".[4] Beyond providing an area for leisure and relaxation, the glacis as the location of numerous markets and storehouses played a role in the city's economic life.

The fortification walls themselves remained untouched. The technically obsolete defensive line had however failed their most recent test: In 1809, Napoleon's troops blew up large portions of the walls between Kärntner Tor and Schottentor gates. Nonetheless, Emperor Franz I (II) had them rebuilt by 1817, with their location shifted in the area of the Hofburg to create space for Heldenplatz, Burggarten and Volksgarten, as well as for Peter von Nobile's new Burgtor. The intention was to maintain, at least symbolically, the function of the city's walls. The military was the owner of the valuable property on the glacis. Obtaining its consent for development of the enormous area was made even more difficult because of the emergence of an internal threat with the revolution of 1848. Now the army insisted with yet greater vehemence on upholding a general ban on construction in the area. After the revolution's suppression, the *ancien régime* was revived under the banner of neo-absolutism, which did not however eradicate the revolutionary potential. The miserable social situation of day labourers and workmen, as well as intolerable living conditions endured by a substantial portion of the capital's population remained unchanged. It was thus logical that in response to the latent internal threat, the military's influence on constitution, legislation and administration of the neo-absolutist regime reached its apogee. Just as the army had first opposed de-fortification of the city, because of the peril posed by foreign foes, it now vigorously championed realisation of old plans for the construction of barracks. Outside the city to the south, and at both ends of Franz-Josef Kai, strategic bases were to be established. The Arsenal was constructed in 1849–56 as the first section in this triangular ring of fortifications. The building of the Franz-Josef-Kaserne on the Dominikanerbastei was to follow in 1854–57. Together with the Rossauer Kaserne, which was completed in 1870, this system was designed to enable the military to hold the capital as though in a pincers.

New public edifices could thus be built only in the suburbs, on whose outskirts a compact built-up area had grown up by mid-century. The state of urban development thus reflected a social separation between suburbs and city proper, which was dominated by the aristocracy and haute bourgeoisie. In 1852, before construction of the two barracks inside the city, the youthful Emperor Franz Josef launched the "New Vienna" project in the face of opposition from mainstream opinion then dominated by military interests. A new district comprising six city blocks was to be established on a small part of the glacis between Währinger Strasse and Danube Canal. The army gave its assent, as a strip of the glacis would remain unaffected by the plan. A financing model was adopted for this novel undertaking that five years later would be employed for the much more ambitious Ringstrasse project. Revenues from the sale and auction of new building lots were used to set up a fund which was at the exclusive disposition of the imperial house for major construction projects in the city and its environs. The sale of real estate properties however proceeded slowly, and in 1858, even as the Ringstrasse was being planned, the plots had yet to be completely developed.

Following a failed attempt to assassinate Emperor Franz Josef on 18 February 1853, his brother, Archduke Ferdinand Max appealed to the "peoples of the monarchy" to finance "in spiritual atonement for the criminal act in Vienna", construction of a church suitable to the purpose.[5] Some 300,000 citizens responded to the appeal for donations. The competition for the commission for the new church was won by Heinrich Ferstel with a Neo-Gothic design, but only in 1855 was a location decided upon. The military's construction ban for the Alser glacis was lifted by *Allerhöchstes*

Cabinetsschreiben (Imperial Cabinet Decree), and construction of the Votivkirche, which was characterised by "Strict Historicism", began in April 1856. Ferstel's Neo-Gothic design marked the end of early Viennese historicism, whose final anachronistic echo was to be the Imperial Opera (1861–69). The opera with its detail of structure and dry, graphic style of its façade was destined to be an artistic failure.

On 20 December 1857, Franz Josef I sent the much quoted handwritten note to his interior minister, Alexander von Bach, which put an end to decades of debate and marked the beginning of Vienna's "Ringstrasse Era". The Emperor wrote:

"It is my will that the enlargement of the inner city of Vienna, taking into account the connection of the former with its suburbs, be taken in hand as soon as possible, whereby the regulation and beautification of my residence and imperial capital shall also be given due regard. To this end I grant permission for demolition of the walls and fortifications of the inner city, as well as the trenches of the same". In addition, the Emperor instructed that, "construction [...] of the necessary buildings for museums and galleries [...] should be taken into consideration".[6]

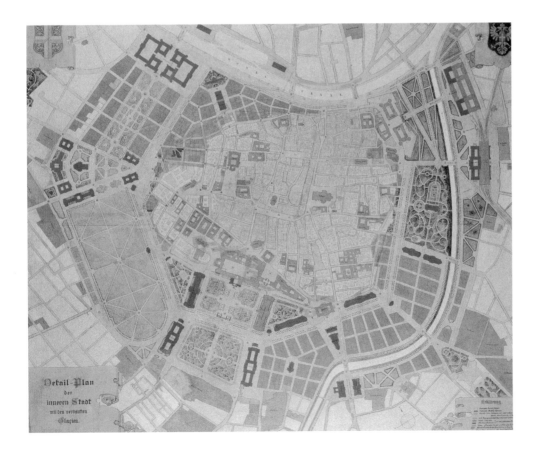

August Sicard von Sicardsburg and Eduard van der Nüll, "Projekt für die Umgestaltung der k. k. Residenzstadt nach Abtragung der Wälle, Detail-Plan", 1858. Wien Museum, Inv. No. 31.010 (© Wien Museum).

An invitation for submissions to a competition for a "Master Plan" *(Grundplan)* for the city was issued on 30 January 1858. By July of the same year, eighty-five projects had been entered. The architectural firms of Sicardsburg/van der Null, Ludwig Förster, and Friedrich Stache tied for first place. The plan was obvious because it had by necessity to take as orientation the old ring of fortifications. In compliance with the numerous stipulations of the competition, the participating architects divided the polygon of streets in front of the former fortifications with streets and squares positioned at right angles, and integrated the planned monumental buildings into this scheme.

Differences between the various plans were to be found in the varying balance between Ringstrasse and side streets, street dimensions and green areas, developed

August Sicard von Sicardsburg and Eduard van der Null, "Projekt für die Umgestaltung der k. k. Residenzstadt nach Abtragung der Wälle", 1858. "Isometrische Projection verschiedener Stadttheile", detail. Wien Museum, Inv. No. 31.013 (© Wien Museum).

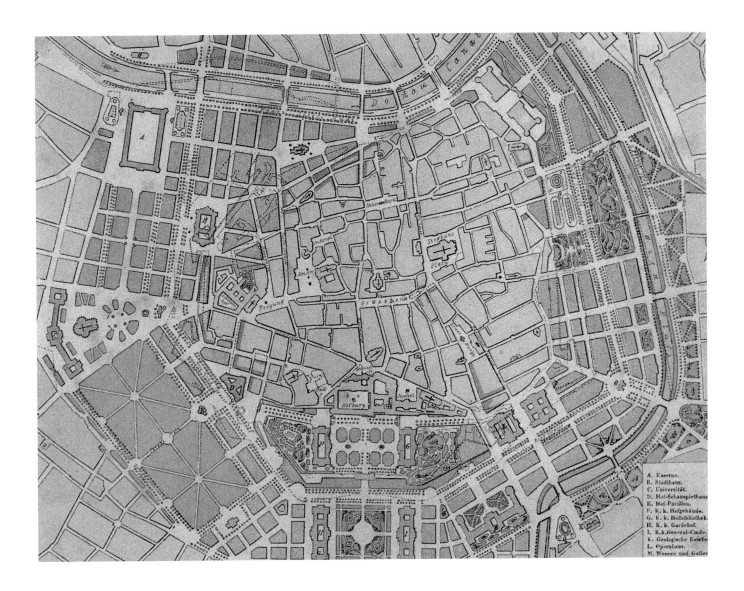

The *Grundplan* or Master Plan, 1859. Wien Museum, Inv. No. 67.989 (© Wien Museum).

and vacant zones. Sicardsburg and van der Nüll and Stache foresaw the Ringstrasse running uniformly around the city. Förster in contrast planned the boulevard to gradually narrow in front of the Hofburg, so that it merged into the general street network before reaching the parade grounds (today the location of Parliament, City Hall and University), which was originally required by the invitation to tender. Stache planned a higher proportion of green areas. In connection with the museum project, it may be noted that Sicardsburg and van der Nüll, who were Hasenauer's instructors at the Academy, envisaged one museum on the northwest side of Heldenplatz on the grounds of the Volksgarten and another on the southwest, extending into the Burggarten. New edifices for the army's headquarters and guard house were to be located on the axis that ran slightly outwards on Bellariastrasse and Babenbergerstrasse respectively. In so doing they anticipated in a rudimentary manner Semper's plan for the Kaiserforum, or Imperial Forum. Other architects proposed situating the planned cultural institutions between Schwarzenbergplatz and Stadtpark (Förster), at the intersection of Währingerstrasse and Schottenring (Kink), near Bellariastrasse (Lenné), on the southern side of Opernring (Löhr), or on the southeast side of Getreidemarkt (Zettl). Based on the three winning entries, a commission, of which the aforementioned architects were also members, agreed the Master Plan, which was approved on 1 September 1859; this plan was subsequently to be modified in several significant respects. The Master Plan envisaged a uniformly broad Ringstrasse, which merged at both ends into Franz-Josef-Kai; buildings for the Imperial Court and Imperial Library were to be located opposite the Hofburg on Heldenplatz. At a right angle to the Ringstrasse and at the axis of the two aforementioned buildings, between Ringstrasse and the Imperial Stables, were the "k. k. Gardehof" and "k. k. Gardekommando" or "k. k. Stadtkommandatur", the military headquarters for the capital – a variant of the proposals made by Sicardsburg and van der Null. In addition, on what is today Schillerplatz, there were to be "museums and galleries". The opera was to be situated at the location eventually chosen, whilst where the Museum of Applied Arts now stands "market halls" were planned. The "Hof-Schauspielhaus" (Imperial Theatre) was to be located where it is today, and behind the Votivkirche then under construction, the university, the "Stadthaus" or municipal building where the stock exchange is now located, and finally a barracks (later Rossauer Kaserne) on Franz-Josef-Kai. The area eventually to be the location of Parliament, City Hall and University was to be left undeveloped for use as parade grounds. This plan was intended to satisfy state and private needs for representation and secure the economic benefits of optimised transportation routes. At this time it was still believed that social and housing crises would be ameliorated, at least indirectly. Although it was not expected that cheaper accommodations would be available in the newly constructed buildings, it was hoped that the relocation of more affluent classes from suburbs to areas along the new boulevard would release reasonably priced living quarters in the surrounding districts. At the same time, factory owners were called upon to construct apartments and housing estates for their workers.

The circumstance that most of the properties had been under state control for decades, and the conditions attached to revenues obtained from their use prevented large-scale speculation and the attendant danger of the overall plan being mangled. The military was largely expropriated and ownership of the glacis transferred to the civil administration (Zivilärar). The property rights were then made over to the Municipal Extension Fund (Stadterweiterungsfonds). The interior ministry was also included in the process through the Vienna Building Commission, a body over which it exercised control. Finally, the Municipal Extension Fund administered sale of the building lots. Not subject to this process were construction projects which lay within the responsibility of the municipality, i.e. construction of the new City Hall, streets, regulation of the Wien river, building of bridges and the like. A project of such dimensions gave rise to periodic disputes between the city authorities and Municipal Extension Fund, the cause of which were purportedly ambiguous property claims. The conflicts were ended in the early 1890s with the Fund's exclusion from all matters related to municipal planning. The later division of the Stuben district into lots and the "second municipal extension" was carried out by the city authorities alone.[7]

Demolition of the bastions commenced in March 1858. Individual calls for tender were then issued, the first of which was for the Court Opera. The design submitted by the architects Sicardsburg and van der Nüll, that is the firm that had worked on the Master Plan, won the competition. Even as the building was under construction in 1861–69, the previously mentioned shift from Early Historicism to Strict Historicism took place, and made this, the first of the Ringstrasse's monumental edifices, a publicly lambasted failure. Opposite the opera, Heinrich Drasche-Wartinberg, the owner of a brick factory, financed construction of an enormous apartment building with a covered arcade for shops, which was known as Heinrichshof (Theophil Hansen, 1860–65; demolished after 1945). At the same time, on what was to become Schwarzenbergplatz, a series of private buildings went up, including the Palais Ludwig Victor (today: Burgtheater, Kasino am Schwarzenbergplatz). The palaces erected for members of the imperial house, the Deutschmeisterpalais and Palais Württemberg, were to act as an impulse for middle class building activities. The location for the equestrian statute of Prince Karl Philipp Schwarzenberg (1771–1820) was also determined, and with it the focal point of the future square. Later, in 1873, on the occasion of the completion of the first aqueduct supplying the capital with water from the Alps, the Hochstrahlbrunnen, a large fountain, was added.

As early as 1833 Josef Calasanz von Arneth, curator and subsequently director of the Imperial Coin and Antiquities Cabinet, had called for the imperial collections to be exhibited to the public at a single location. The works of art were no longer mere curiosities but "a medium of instruction and education".[8] In the years that followed, plans to build a museum near the Baroque Imperial Library proved abortive, while small regional museums opened in Graz (1811), Prague (1818), Innsbruck (1821), Linz (1833), Salzburg (1834) and Klagenfurt (1846). It was only as part of the capital's extension that realisation of the museum project – already some twenty years old – came within reach. The conditions, both as to space and finances, now existed to permit presentation of the imperial collections in an appropriate, new edifice built specifically for the purpose and equipped with modern picture hanging and engineering technology. In 1867, the call for proposals for the museums entered a decisive phase. It may be recalled that the Master Plan had foreseen museums and galleries on what is today Schillerplatz. In the meantime ten years had elapsed. Franz Josef I had early on reserved to himself the prerogative of disposing of the area between Imperial Palace and Imperial Stables. In 1864, the Imperial Court real-located the area, which had originally been intended as the location of the military administration. Now museums were "to be constructed on either side of the square between the outer Burgtor and Imperial Stables in two separate buildings, one of which is to house the collections of art and the other, those of natural history".[9]

The Architects

Gottfried Semper (1803–79)

The Hamburg-born architect, university professor and scholar Gottfried Semper was recognized throughout Europe in the middle and second half of the nineteenth century as an authority on monumental architecture in the historical revival style. As such he was also consulted in disputes arising in connection with architectural competitions.[10] Semper started studying mathematics at Göttingen in 1823. Two years later, bowing to his parents' wishes, he applied for admission to engineering school. While waiting to start his new studies, the twenty-two year old travelled to Munich, where he took part in an architecture course given by Friedrich von Gärtner, and subsequently went on to Paris by way of Heidelberg and Regensburg. Here he gained his first impressions at Franz Christian Gau's architecture school before returning to northern Germany. Keeping his engineering studies at the back of his mind, Semper worked for a year at Bremerhaven harbour to acquire practical experience. It was only after this that he definitively decided to pursue the study of architecture. Semper then returned to Paris, where he became Gau's most promising student.

After the July Revolution of 1830 the young architect departed France for the south of the continent. Inspired by the hotly disputed question of the polychrome decoration of ancient buildings, in which Jacques-Ignace Hittorf in Paris played a leading role, Semper and his companions extended their travels to Greece. They were eventually to find sufficient evidence that all the major elements of Ancient Greek temples – columns, pediment and base areas, and decorative sculpture – had originally been painted in a variety of colours. With the publication of these findings in 1834 Semper took part in a decisive manner in the scholarly debate, and delivered a spectacular refutation of the ideal postulated by Winckelmann and Goethe of the "noble simplicity and silent grandeur" of Greek architecture and sculpture. In the very same year he received his first independent commission to build the Villa

Gottfried Semper, c. 1866. Wien Museum, Inv. No. 213.777 (© Wien Museum).

Donner near Hamburg (damaged in 1942 and subsequently demolished). As it happened, this was also the first museum that Semper realised, for his client had desired a small museum and observatory. It was at this time that Semper, upon Gau's recommendation, became a professor at the academy in Dresden and thereby an employee of the Saxon court. Semper initiated reforms at the academy, introducing courses in architectural history and promoted a closer relation of theory to practice. He also complemented the traditional system of instruction – in which students were divided into classes according to when they had started their studies – by an atelier, in which beginners and advanced students studied together. In 1835, Semper remodelled the interior of the Japanese Palace erected in 1717 and 1727–33, adding exhibition halls in an antique style for the display of collections of art, antiquities, and coins. In 1838, with the support of Schinkel, who he had met on several occasions in Berlin, he took part in the competition for the design of the Dresden Court Theatre, the predecessor of today's Semper Opera. The execution of his proposal (the theatre opened in 1841) attracted considerable attention owing to its Neo-Renaissance style, which at the time was still unusual. The rigorous logical coherence of the design set new stylistic standards for the future. There followed further commissions in Dresden, Villa Rosa (1838, destroyed 1945), Palais Oppenheim (1848, destroyed 1945), synagogue (1840, destroyed 1938), and finally the Royal Picture Gallery in connection with a project for a forum, which was to remain unexecuted (see chapter on Imperial Forum below).

During the March Revolution of 1848–49 Semper rallied to the revolutionary cause. He belonged to the Academic Division of the Dresden civil militia, and was a member of a sharp-shooting company. In 1849, together with Richard Wager, then Hofkapellmeister, Semper took part in preparations for the general arming of the population. In early May he was commissioned by the provisional government to reinforce a strategically important but inadequately secured barricade, which became known as the Semper Barricade. Prussian troops eventually crushed the rebellion in Dresden and elsewhere and with it the hopes of bourgeois and intellectual circles for a united Germany. The architect, against whom an arrest warrant had been issued, was forced to leave his wife and children behind in Saxony and flee by a risky and circuitous route to Paris. His house in Dresden, the greater part of his property, and his professional and social standing were lost. Semper seriously considered emigrating to the United States. At literally the last moment however he abandoned these plans for what he believed more promising prospects in London. Without steady employment, Semper dedicated himself to his theoretical treatise. Semper met Richard Wagner in Paris, and the composer again championed the architect. It was probably upon his recommendation that Semper was invited to

Zurich for discussions in the autumn of 1854. He was to take on direction of the architecture department of the newly established Polytechnic (today: ETH). After some hesitation, the fifty-two year old Semper agreed in January 1855. But precisely at this moment a larger commission in London seemed finally to take shape. Semper completed plans and models for the Victoria and Albert complex in South Kensington. However, the project was postponed because of a lack of funds, and the commission later given to other architects.

Eventually, Semper moved to Zurich in summer 1855. He won a number of important commissions in Switzerland: new buildings for the Polytechnic in Zurich (1860–62), Zurich observatory (1862), Winterthur city hall (1865). Other projects remained unrealised, the Rio de Janeiro theatre (1858) and Munich Festspielhaus (1866). He had in the meantime firmly established his architecture school. In Zurich he continued the method of instruction he had practiced in Dresden, involving his students in work on his architectural projects. In this way, a circle of Semper's students developed, whose influence made itself felt beyond his lifetime.

In 1868, Carl von Hasenauer first established contact with his more senior colleague in Zurich, requesting help with his submission for the competition for the imperial museums (see chapter "The Competition for the Imperial Museums" below). This signalled the last phase of Semper's work, during which he could look forward to having achieved acceptance of his long pursued project for a monumental forum. Indeed, it was only after his death in 1879 that signs of the project's partial demise began to appear on the horizon. Having left Zurich to supervise implementation of the major undertaking in Vienna, Semper's Dresden period caught up with him in dramatic fashion. He learned from a newspaper article of the destruction by fire of his Court Theatre. The building had burned to its foundations on 21 September 1869. Construction of the new opera house (1871 ff.), today known as the Semper Opera, was led by his son Manfred and completed in 1877 shortly after Gottfried Semper had left Vienna. In 1876 he had been removed from responsibility for the Imperial Forum following a dispute with Hasenauer, which had been fought out in the courts.

Semper likely remained for a few more months in Vienna before spending the winter of 1876–77 in Venice. On 15 May 1879 he died in Rome.

Kaspar von Zumbusch, Gottfried Semper. Marble bust in the staircase of Kunsthistorisches Museum.

Carl von Hasenauer (1833–94)

Carl von Hasenauer, Wien Museum, Inv. No. 194.991 (© Wien Museum).

During his studies at the Academy of Visual Arts in Vienna Carl Hasenauer came into contact with the architectural duo of August Sicard von Sicardsburg (1813–68) and Eduard van der Nüll (1812–68), who were to oversee his education in the years 1850–55.[11] Hasenauer was born in Vienna in 1833 as the son of a Hofzimmermeister, or master carpenter to the imperial court. While a student, Hasenauer undertook trips to northern Italy and Germany, and also visited London and Paris. Some years later in 1861, he took part in the competition for the Court Opera (today: Vienna State Opera), as did his former professors. Hasenauer achieved third place, whilst Sicardsburg and van der Nüll received the commission. However, neither of the winners would witness the prestigious building's inauguration ceremony. Vicious criticism of the nearly completed opera house, in which finally the emperor himself was to join, drove the deeply aggrieved van der Nüll to take his life in 1868. His friend and colleague died just a few weeks later, albeit from natural causes. Hasenauer first received a number of smaller commissions such as those for the former Lindenhof (Geroldgasse 7, in Vienna's seventeenth district) for publisher Moritz Gerold in 1861, and in 1867 for the Austro-Hungarian pavilion at the Paris Universal Exhibition. Initially only Theophil Hansen, Heinrich Ferstel and Moriz Löhr were called upon to submit proposals for the two court museums. Hasenauer presumably intervened behind the scenes to be invited to take part, for it was only later that he was asked to enter a submission (see chapter "The Competition for the Imperial Museums"). Finally, however, the building commission which had developed into a project for the Imperial Forum was entrusted to Hasenauer and Semper. The new Hofburgtheater (opened 1888) had originally been envisaged as occupying a site on the grounds of the Volksgarten and adjoining the Hofburg complex. This was changed in 1870 to a location across the City Hall (completed 1883). Hasenauer was a member of the committee jury for the City Hall project in 1869. He took a particular interested in the theatre's interior decoration. The plans for the building's exterior had been made under Semper's direction.

Hasenauer carried out a relatively small project, the Palais Lützow (1870; Bösendorferstrasse 13, Vienna District I), before construction commenced on the two museums in the autumn of 1871. During the first years of the ambitious project Hasenauer was in charge of another major commission. As chief architect of the Vienna World Exhibition of 1873 he was responsible for supervising construction of more than 130 pavilions for exhibits as well as for catering and entertainment establishments. In recognition of this achievement Hasenauer was raised to the nobility.

In 1877, six years after work on the museums had started, Semper departed Vienna in the wake of a dispute. Hasenauer, who had in the previous year been given a contract for technical management of the project, was now also given its artistic direction. In 1882, a year after construction of the Neue Burg had commenced, Hasenauer received a further imperial commission, for the planning of the Hermesvilla. The palace-like villa situated in the eastern part of the Lainzer Tiergarten was a gift from Franz Josef to his wife Elisabeth. The Hermesvilla remains today an important document of imperial domestic living. The painters Franz Matsch, Ernst and Gustav Klimt co-operated on the villa's interior decoration, as they were later to do for Kunsthistorisches Museum.

In 1884, Hasenauer became a professor at the Academy of Visual Arts and in 1892, two years before his death, was named the institution's rector. The group of monuments which he designed also date to this period: Tegetthoff Monument (1886; Praterstern, Vienna), Maria Theresia Monument (1888; between the two court museums), and Grillparzer Monument (1889; Volksgarten, Vienna).

Viktor Tilgner, Carl von Hasenauer.
Bronze bust in the staircase of
Kunsthistorisches Museum.

Letter from Hasenauer to Semper concerning promise of funding for construction of the Imperial Forum, 21. 7. 1869, ETH Zurich, gta Archives (© ETH Zurich, gta Archives).

The Competition for the Court Museums, 1867–70

Chronology

27 March 1867

First plan by Hasenauer

12 July 1868

Second plan by Hasenauer

4 August 1868

First letter from Hasenauer to Semper

13 October 1868

The directors of the collection indicate their preference for Hasenauer's plan

15 January 1869

The Imperial Household officially charges Semper with producing an expertise

11 March 1869

Semper completes his expertise
"Report Concerning the Assessment and Comparison of Two Projects for the Construction of the New Imperial Royal Museums in Vienna"

April 1869

Audience of Semper with Emperor Franz Josef I
Commission awarded orally

From April 1869

Semper cooperates with Hasenauer in Zurich in drawing up the first plans

Late July 1870

Commission awarded in writing to Semper and Hasenauer

Vienna had by now become one of the grand European stages for modern architecture. Architects Theophil Hansen,[15] Heinrich Ferstel,[16] Moritz Löhr,[17] and finally Carl Hasenauer too, were invited to submit entries for what was perhaps the most prestigious architectural project. In their plans both Hansen and Ferstel self-confidently ignored the terms of the call for proposals. The imperial client had stipulated that two separate museums be constructed. Both architects accepted the Ringstrasse as the outer edge of the project and conceived the museum as an independent complex detached from the buildings of the Hofburg. Hansen designed his museums in "Greco-Renaissance Style",[18] thereby reverting to an idiom which had been *de rigueur* for museum buildings prior to the Alte Pinakothek in Munich (1836). Soon thereafter, without a competition being held, Hansen was charged with construction of the parliament building. Ferstel was to receive commissions for the Museum of Art and Industry (today: the Austrian Museum of Applied Arts) in 1871, the School

Theophil Hansen, "Entwurf für die neu zu erbauenden k. k. Museen in Wien", 1867. Wien Museum, Inv. No. 19.930 (© Wien Museum).

Heinrich Ferstel, "Museen für Kunst- und Naturwissenschaftliche Sammlungen". 1867. Wien Museum, Inv. No. 164311/1 (© Wien Museum).

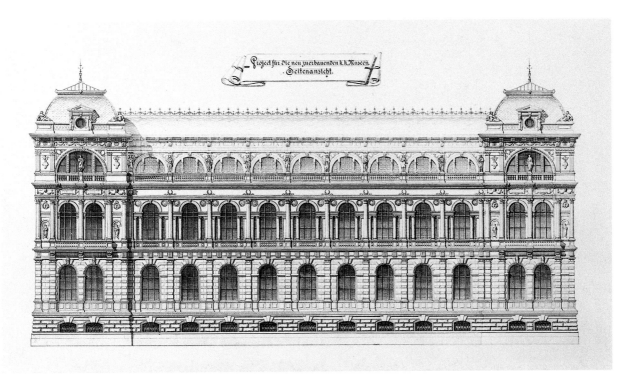

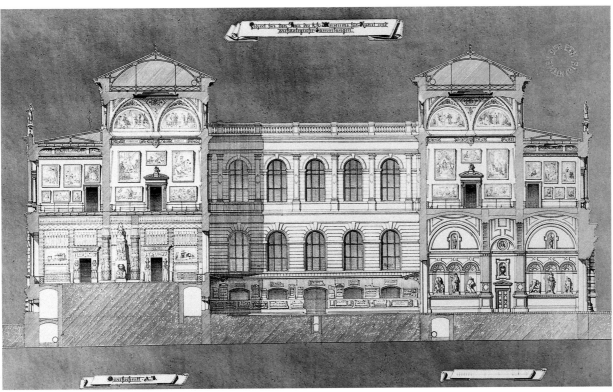

Carl Hasenauer, first plan for the museums, side view and cross section, A–B, 1867, ETH Zurich, gta Archives (© ETH Zurich, gta Archiv).

Carl Hasenauer, first plan for the museums, bird's eye view in the direction of the imperial stables, 1867. Vienna, Österreichisches Haus-, Hof- und Staatsarchiv, Planarchiv (© Österreichisches Haus-, Hof- und Staatsarchiv).

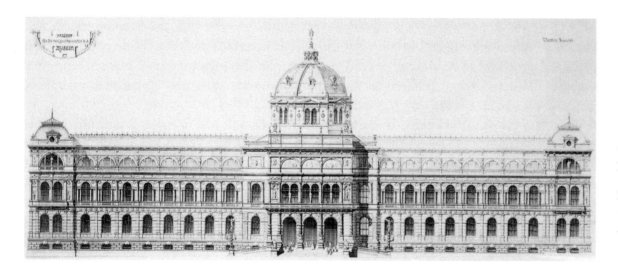

Carl Hasenauer, first plan for the museums, 1867. Zurich. ETH Zurich, gta Archives). (© ETH Zurich, gta Archives).

Carl Hasenauer, first plan for the museums, façade facing Babenbergerstrasse, 1867. ETH Zurich, gta Archiv (© ETH Zurich, gta Archives).

of Industrial Arts (today: the University of Applied Arts) in 1877, and finally the main building of Vienna University (1883).

In the design submitted to the competition – apparently without being invited to do so – Hasenauer defined major parameters for the buildings, which were maintained in the structures that he later realized together with Semper. There were to be "two courtyards for light and air" with an entryway for vehicles from the street, "in order that art objects, goods [and] heating materials could be delivered to the museum avoiding the public entrance". On the ground floor were to be "apartments for the house inspector, concierge, janitor, as well as for four servants, eight menials, and stokers", as well as the "picture storeroom". Above were to be "a high floor on the ground level and the first floor". The building bordering on what is today Babenbergerstrasse was to become the Kunsthistorisches Museum, so that the "cabinets for the Italian and Spanish Schools have a northern exposure". Visitors would enter the museum "over a large flight of stairs and ramp [...] to an entrance hall, and thence over several steps to a vestibule; through large sliding doors to a massive staircase above which rises a cupola, whose windows illuminate the staircase".

In the courtyard area, the arcades which according to the architect were customary in Renaissance palaces were dispensed with, for they "robbed the windows of light". Each area of the collections was to receive exhibition rooms of different proportions. The director's room was to be located on the same floor as his collection. For the rooms housing the Egyptian collection, Hasenauer proposed columns with "lotus bud capitals"; not yet under consideration were the authentic papyrus columns that

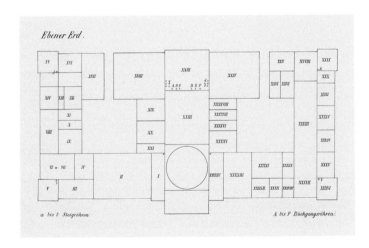

Floor plan "Ebener Erd", first plan from: Carl Hasenauer, *Erläuternde Denkschrift über sein Project für die neu zu erbauenden k. k. Museen*, Vienna, 1867.

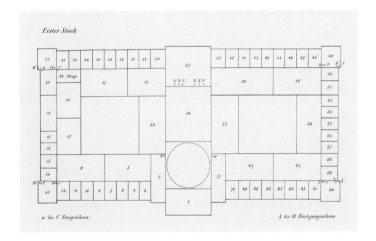

Floor plan "Erster Stock", first plan from Carl Hasenauer, *Erläuternde Denkschrift über sein Project für die neu zu erbauenden k. k. Museen*, Vienna, 1867.

were eventually installed. In the same manner, decorative elements inspired by classical antiquity were to be employed in the galleries for these collections, and a medieval style for those in which the collection of arms and armour were to be displayed. The rooms were to be differently proportioned. At this stage the architect's design was more clearly oriented to the structure and size of the various collections than was to be case in the final plan.

In the Picture Gallery the cabinets were to be fitted with the largest possible windows so as "to prevent hard shadows". In addition, it was to be possible to transport paintings by lift from the storeroom to a number of galleries equipped with a "trapdoor in the floor", thus eliminating the necessity of moving the artworks over the stairways. The "fatigued public" was to be able to withdraw to the "salons" and "revive themselves with fresh air" on the adjoining balconies. The cleverly devised floor plan would permit visitors "to wander through the galleries in a circular fashion without interruption". The lighting of the exhibition rooms was to be assured by skylights. To protect the paintings from damage, it was proposed that "barricades" be installed around the galleries which could also function as heating pipes. Finally, fans would be required inside the building to prevent larger accumulations of dust. Outside, the same purpose would be served by large lawns and fountains.

The exterior was to "appear monumental at first glance" and make a "serene yet not overly solemn impression". Through the broad flight of stairs and "high arch" the museum would be "open to all" and "beckon to visit". Hasenauer moved the cupola from the centre of the building towards Maria Theresien-Platz with a view to constructing a visual relationship with the second museum opposite. This is thus another characteristic of the completed building that was determined by Hasenauer. The building was given a "massive base area" as well as four corner structures with balconies, behind which the "salons" were located. The façade was lent the necessary calm by "continuous horizontal lines", whilst the first floor was adorned "more richly with columns" and restrained ornament with cartouches inscribed with artists' names, portrait medallions, and above the cabinets, statues of artists located in front of the skylights.[19]

Representative of the lively public discourse surrounding the project is a critique published by Rudolf von Eitelberger shortly after the first competition in December 1867.[20] The art historian and founder of the Museum for Art and Industry, which was established in 1864, questioned the formal equality of the two museum buildings. A natural history collection, in his view, demanded "an entirely different type" of building than a collection of art. The new art museum should not be any less "magnificent and opulent" than the Upper Belvedere palace. He thus proposed that design of the museum of natural history be entrusted to a different architect. As to style, and in connection with his call to extend or complete Fischer von Erlach's plans for the Hofburg, Eitelberger championed a Neo-Baroque approach. This was long before the Neo-Baroque, the final phase of Viennese Historicism, took hold. Eitelberger at this date thus already indirectly proposed construction of the complex which in the guise of the Imperial Forum Semper was later to help to a breakthrough, although the grand project was destined to remain uncompleted.

Carl Hasenauer, second plan for Kunsthistorisches Museum, 1868. Zurich, ETH Zurich, gta Archives (© ETH Zurich, gta Archives).

Carl Hasenauer, second plan for the museums, drawn in perspective, 1868. ETH Zurich, gta Archives (© ETH Zurich, gta Archives).

Carl Hasenauer, second plan
for Kunsthistorisches Museum,
façade facing Babenbergerstrasse, dated 10 May 1869.
ETH Zurich, gta Archives
(© ETH Zurich, gta Archives).

The disparate imperial art collections were to be presented to the public in a "clear and well structured fashion", in surroundings offering adequate seating and good catalogues. In contrast to and entirely differently from its companion institution, the museum of natural history, the art museum was to be endowed with the appearance of a scientific institution, for "more than books, it is paintings and art objects that stimulate patriotism". Eitelberger desired the inclusion in the art museum of an "Imperial Hall" adorned with portraits of "all the Habsburg rulers of Austria arranged in chronological order and executed by the most outstanding artists of the day". This idea reappeared in adapted form in the decoration of the cupola hall of the finished building.

In his critique, Eitelberger repeatedly appealed for the museums neither to be designed in a style foreign to the place and antipathetic to the Viennese mentality, nor executed by a foreign architect. In the same year Eitelberger had requested Semper's expertise in connection with the construction of his own institution, the Museum for Art and Industry, and much valued his professional judgement. In 1867, Semper dedicated to Eitelberger a copy of his manuscript of *The Ideal Museum. Practical Art in Metals and Hard Materials*. The work, which he had completed in London in 1852,[21] contains an organizational plan for a model museum of applied arts, where objects would be displayed according to the techniques used to create them, for example, weaving or pottery.

To return to the competition in Vienna however, the jury members and contractor were for several months unable to agree on one or other of the

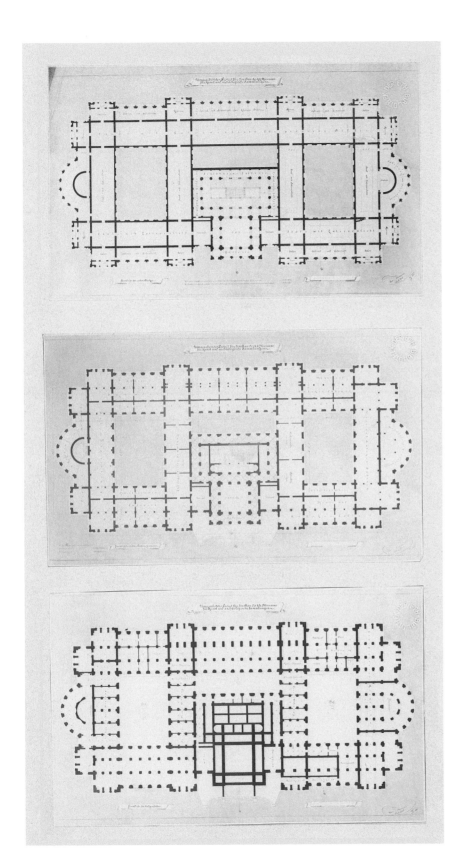

Carl Hasenauer, second plan for Kunsthistorisches Museum, floor plans, dated
10 May 1869. ETH Zurich, gta Archives
(© ETH Zurich, gta Archives).

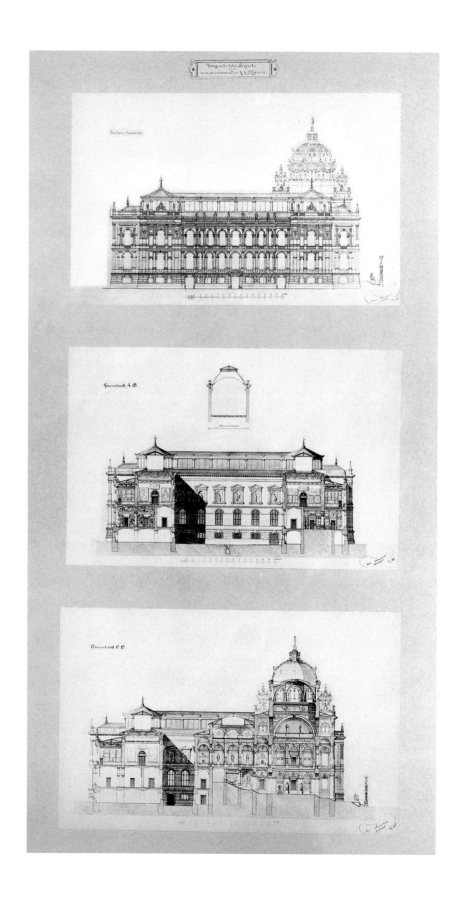

Carl Hasenauer, second plan for Kunsthistorisches Museum, façade facing Burgring
and cross sections, 1868, ETH Zurich, gta
Archives (© ETH Zurich, gta Archives).

46

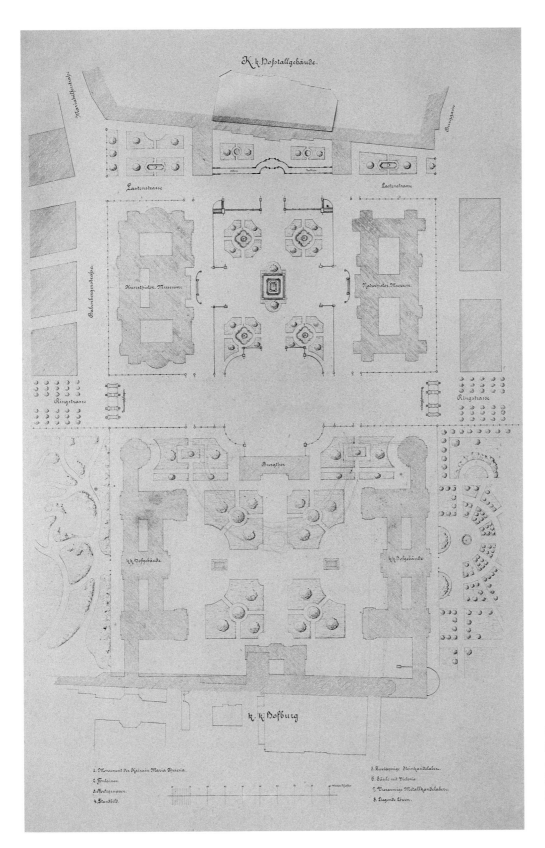

Carl Hasenauer, second plan for the museums, site plan, dated 18 May 1869. ETH Zurich, gta Archives (© ETH Zurich, gta Archives).

Moriz von Löhr, second plan for the museums, 1868. Wien Museum, Inv. No. 76.219 (© Wien Museum).

projects. Responding to public pressure, all four participants in the competition were given the opportunity to make changes to their proposals; in the event only Hasenauer and Löhr did so. Hansen suggested drawing on the services of an external consultant. Meanwhile Hasenauer had modified his entry. Insofar as may be surmised from the surviving plans, the new proposal differed from the first in two important respects. Although the architect did not change the position of the dome, he did move the staircase to the building's centre. The "necessary serenity of the façade", which he had previously championed, now gave way to ornament with pronounced sculptural features. In a certain way Hasenauer seems thus to have responded to the authoritarian criticism expressed by Eitelberger, who in his memorandum called for the building to reflect the Austrian architecture of the Baroque. The silhouette of this "pavilion architecture", as Semper was later to characterise it, indeed recalls the Upper Belvedere palace.

In the meantime, Hasenauer's sole remaining competitor, Moriz von Löhr emerged as the winner of the competition. The jury judged his proposal to be the most functional of those submitted and recommended its execution. The jury's verdict was however not based on a firmly held conviction and eventually proved abortive. The Austrian Association of Engineers and Architects championed the first – and only – plan entered by Hansen. Hasenauer attempted to take advantage of jury member Eduard von der Null's death on 4 April 1868, i.e. before the decision in favour of Löhr, and unaware of the appointment of Johannes Rösner. On 4 August 1868, Hasenauer turned for the first time to Semper, who earlier that year had become a member of the Vienna Academy of Arts and been in Vienna on earlier occasions. Hasenauer asked him to assume von der Null's place on the jury. Meanwhile, prominent members of the Austrian Association of Engineers and Architects had used their influence to have Semper named to the jury while Hansen lobbied for his appointment at an audience with the emperor. Thus was the award of the contract to Löhr, which had already been drawn up in cabinet, thwarted by public pressure.[22] Until receiving an official note from the Austrian embassy in Bern on 15 January 1869, Semper apparently had not replied to any of Hasenauer's letters. Now the imperial house itself requested Semper to evaluate the latest plans, and appointed him personal counsellor to the emperor. The formal documents arrived in Zurich in late January 1869.

Endowed now with this status Semper drafted his expertise of 11 March 1869 in which he questioned the project specifications *in toto* and thus reiterated Eitelberger's wish that the Hofburg be included in the overall plan.[23] The centre of imperial power enlarged by the museum buildings was also conceived as the Ringstrasse's urban and architectural centrepiece. Semper begins with a general piece of advice: however the square is to be built, the "principal focus of attention should be devoted to the Hofburg remaining or becoming the dominant central point of the entire complex; everything else should be subordinate to and placed in relationship to it". For this reason alone, Hasenauer's "pavilion architecture" with its "many projections and indentations could not be endorsed". The size of the square and building area "required the largest dimensions possible". The buildings should have a great deal of open area on what today are Babenbergerstrasse and Bellariastrasse, in order too to contain the development of dust inside the museums. The "inner harmony of the exhibition rooms" could be achieved "not only [by] differing decoration" but also "adapting the architectural style" to the objects exhibited. This should not, however, be "at the expense of harmony and continuity of access". Here Semper enunciated his frequently quoted judgement about Moriz von Löhr's competing design, whose gallery rooms he found to resemble "a simple goods warehouse" or "artillery depot". Hasenauer had attempted to design the galleries' ornament and interior decoration to reflect their contents, but this as a whole was "at the expense of harmony". For it was "the most difficult challenge to combine this diversity with the equally desired harmony of its parts, and unite them into a whole". Differently from Hasenauer, Semper calls for the strict separation and autonomy of public and non-public areas, in particular in connection with the positioning and number of staircases. The lighting of the galleries by means of skylights was a matter of general agreement, although Semper favoured a different technical solution (see illustrations pp. 221–22).

The use of the cupola involved the architects "in great difficulties". In his second design Hasenauer had placed the staircase behind the cupola, which would thus become visible only from the first floor; the "ground floor vestibule" was to be vaulted. In this way the cupola would "bring to a climax the progression of effects from entrance to the interior of the main floor". Hansen's Renaissance style was "not the chaste, elegant, albeit somewhat anaemic early Renaissance, but rather full and powerful in detail, particularly in the interiors of the rooms". Hence, from this point of view, the old plan with "its Tuscan ground floor and triglyph beams" was deemed preferable. Von Löhr's design, which had been briefly chosen as the winner and was still under consideration, earned an unambiguous verdict from Semper: "fatiguing monotony and sobriety" and "inadequate elaboration of plans". This judgement was sufficient to exclude the architect from the running despite his support in the imperial bureaucracy. Semper concluded, "in my humble opinion the question of the person of the architect is the main point, that is, who is the right man to take on a work of such supreme importance – and however many worthy works they had to their credit, these two could offer no certain criteria". The project was "to be started anew, in particular in connection with a much more comprehensive concept centring on construction of a new imperial residence, to which the two museums must be subordinate. This is not to say that a new palace would have to be built immediately. Nonetheless, the necessary scale, at present in fact completely absent, would thereby be achieved; without this even the greatest of geniuses is deprived of orientation and rudder for his endeavours".

Semper apparently did not reckon with further commissions, for he departed Vienna by way of Berlin for his home town, Altona near Hamburg. There a letter from the Imperial Oberst-kämmerer Count Crenneville reached him. Crenneville asked Semper to return to Vienna as quickly as possible to speak with Franz Josef I. He met the emperor on 6 April at the residence in Buda. Franz Josef wavered still between Hansen and Hasenauer. Semper wrote his son, "I long for the peace and quiet of Zurich; nothing but bothersome honours!".[24] Only after returning to Vienna did the monarch decide to request Semper to present a plan of his own, provided he accepted one of the competition participants as assistant (and thus the latter's plan as the basis for the design). Semper agreed to these terms though he must have suspected that he was thereby venturing onto treacherous terrain. He first contacted his "old friend" Hansen, who declined for reasons of health. Whether he met von Löhr is not known. This option was eliminated in any event after he had been roughly excluded from the competition. Semper was thus compelled to cooperate with Hasenauer, whose decorative talent he "valued exception-ally" notwithstanding his criticism of the latter's plan.[25] During the summer of 1869 Semper busied himself with work on the new plan in Zurich. Hasenauer provided him not only with the necessary technical information, but also related the growing resentment fanned by Löhr of "the foreigner" who had taken from him the much coveted commission. Semper though, was by no means a stranger to Viennese scholarly and artistic circles. While between 1869 and

Seine Excellenz der Herr Oberstkämmerer
Feldzeugmeister Graf Crenneville gaben
Eurer Wohlgeboren bekannt, daß Seine
Apostolische Majestæt der Kaiser und
König Sie morgen, Dienstag den 13. dieses
Monats 12 Uhr Mittags, in Privat Audienz
zu empfangen geruhen werden.

Gleichzeitig werden Eure Wohlgeboren
eingeladen sich behufs weiterer Besprechung
noch vor der Audienz d: i: vor 1/2 12
Uhr im Bureau Seiner Excellenz des Herrn
Oberstkämmerer gefälligst einzufinden.
Wien am 12. April 1869

Vom k. k. Oberstkämmerer-Amte.

Seiner Wohlgeboren
dem Herrn Professor Semper.

Gottfried Semper, first plan for the Kaiser Forum or Imperial Forum. Zurich, 1869. Vienna, Österreichisches Haus-, Hof- und Staatsarchiv, Planarchiv (© Österreichisches Haus-, Hof- und Staatsarchiv).

1871 Semper had visited Vienna but briefly, in 1872 he moved to the city to join his daughter Anna Catherina (1843-1929; Laudongasse 26, Eighth District). When in 1873 she married historian Theodor von Sickel (1826–1908), who had lived in Vienna since 1855, Semper took an apartment of his own at Mölkerbastei 7 in the capital's First District. The Sickels – the historian had taught at the newly established Institute for Austrian Historical Research since 1857 – apparently eased the foreigner's entrance into Viennese society. In the mid-1870's many of Sickel's university colleagues and friends, established scholars and journalists, also belonged Semper's circle of acquaintances. Several visits by Semper to Makart's atelier have been documented; indeed it was here that he again met Richard Wagner in 1875.[26] Semper's plan – floor plan and aerial view – which he completed while still in Zurich shows a monumental court of honour, which was destined to make architectural history as the Imperial Forum. It is clear that the museums as completed and indeed parts of the Kaiserforum plan – Hasenauer's situation plan for the second draft phase already included a triumphal arch spanning the Ringstrasse – were

Gottfried Semper, first plan for the Kaiser Forum or Imperial Forum. Zurich, 1869. Vienna, Österreichisches Haus-, Hof- und Staatsarchiv, Planarchiv (© Österreichisches Haus-, Hof- und Staatsarchiv).

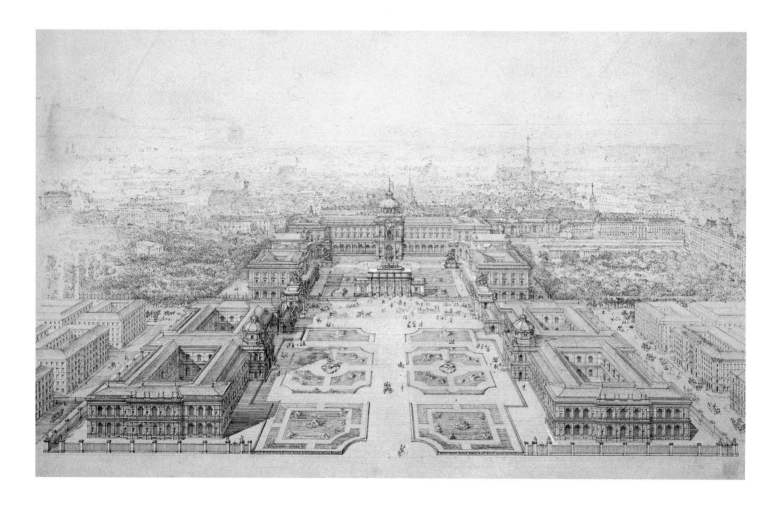

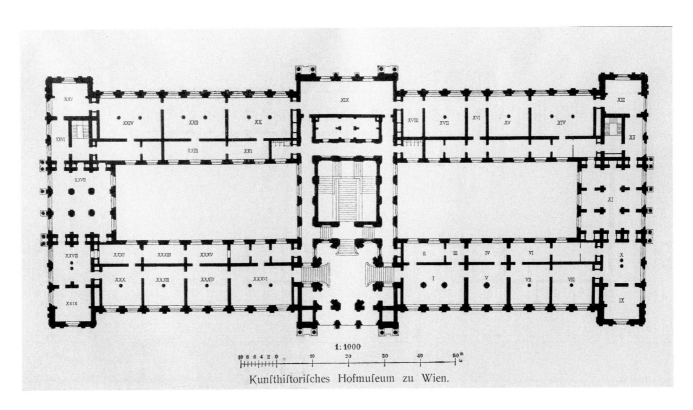

Ground plan Kunsthistorisches Museum, ground floor. Heinrich Wagner, *Handbuch der Architektur,* part 4, vol. 6, fascicle 4: Josef Durm, Hermann Ende (eds.), *Gebäude für Sammlungen und Ausstellungen,* 2nd ed., Stuttgart, 1906, ill. 484.

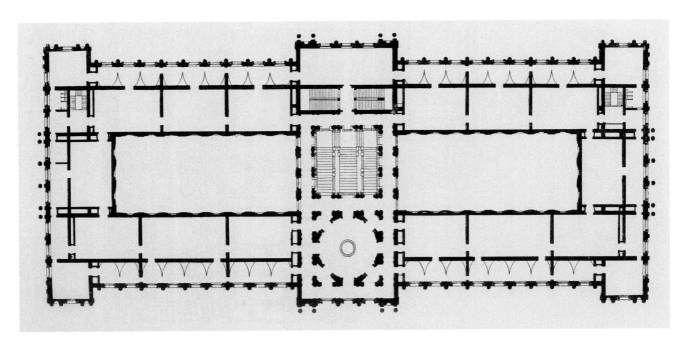

Ground plan Kunsthistorisches Museum, first floor. Heinrich Wagner, *Handbuch der Architektur,* part 4, vol. 6, fascicle 4: Josef Durm, Hermann Ende (eds.), *Gebäude für Sammlungen und Ausstellungen,* 2nd ed., Stuttgart, 1906, ill. 485.

based on these previous designs (Ringstrasse plan by Sicardsburg/van der Nüll, Eitelberger's *Denkschrift*, and of course Hasenauer's plans). Without venturing a comprehensive evaluation of Semper's work, his achievement can be said to lie in particular in unifying, monumentalising and thoroughly imbuing with a logical structure the disparate plans, which had been previously drafted based on different conditions. At the end of July 1870, four years after the establishment of the North German Confederation that cemented the "Lesser German Solution", about half a year before proclamation of the German Empire on 18 January 1871, and four years after the Austro-Hungarian "Compromise", Semper and Hasenauer were officially commissioned with execution of the plans for the two museums, extension of the Hofburg, and Burgtheater. "Dear Count Taaffe! Having resolved to join construction of the museums with the enlargement of My Imperial Palace and theatre, execution of the museums according to the plans of von Löhr is to be abandoned. However, I am not ill-disposed to approve the project drawn up by the architects Semper and Hasenauer in connection with the aforementioned buildings".[27] Construction was set to begin without ceremony on 27 November 1871. In the meantime Semper had received confirmation from Vienna of a lifetime pension, after having been discharged from the Swiss civil service in June. He moved to Vienna and participated in the first meetings of the newly formed Building Committee. As is well-known from anecdotal Viennese social and architectural history, a harmonious working relationship between the two architects did not long prevail. Five years after construction had commenced they communicated with one another

Kunsthistorisches Museum, cross section, 15 January 1871. Vienna, Österreichisches Haus-, Hof- und Staatsarchiv, Planarchiv (© Österreichisches Haus-, Hof- und Staatsarchiv).

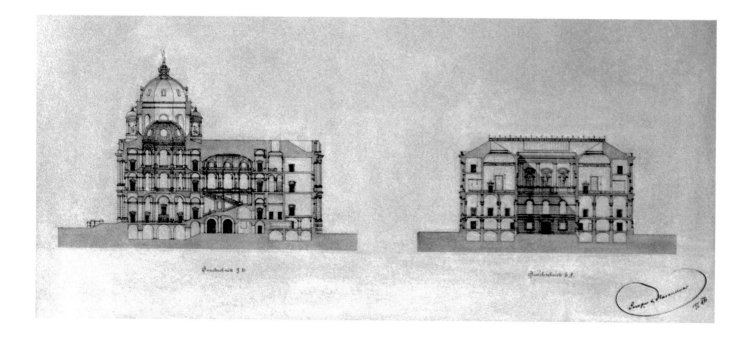

only through their attorneys. In 1877 Hasenauer assumed sole control of construction. This gives rise to questions concerning attribution of individual planning decisions, to which definitive answers are hardly possible, especially as a consequence of Semper's death in 1879. Hasenauer was later inclined to let himself be celebrated as the museums' sole creator, whilst Semper's son, Manfred, and son-in-law, Theodor Sickel, saw themselves compelled to champion publicly the claims of the deceased star architect.

Gottfried Semper and Carl Hasenauer, façades facing Burgring and Maria Theresien-Platz, 1871. ETH Zurich, gta Archives (© ETH Zurich, gta Archives).

Plan: Gottfried Semper, inscription: Carl Hasenauer, partial frontal elevation of façade facing Maria Theresien-Platz showing part of the triumphal arch originally planned to span the Ringstrasse, 1870 (?). ETH Zurich, gta Archives (© ETH Zurich, gta Archives).

DEN DENKMÄLERN DER KVNST VND DES ALTERTHVMES
HAT DIESES MVSEVM ERBAVT KAISER FRANZ JOSEPH I.
IM JAHRE MDCCCLXXIII

K.K.HOFMUSEUMS IN WIEN
SPLAN.)

Druck v. bei Weigel. Wien 1873.

R.v.Waldheim art.Anst.Wien.

Previous double page:
Construction drawing
of the façade of the
museum. Implementa-
tion plan in: Manfred
Semper, *Hasenauer
und Semper,* Hamburg,
1895, sheet 2.

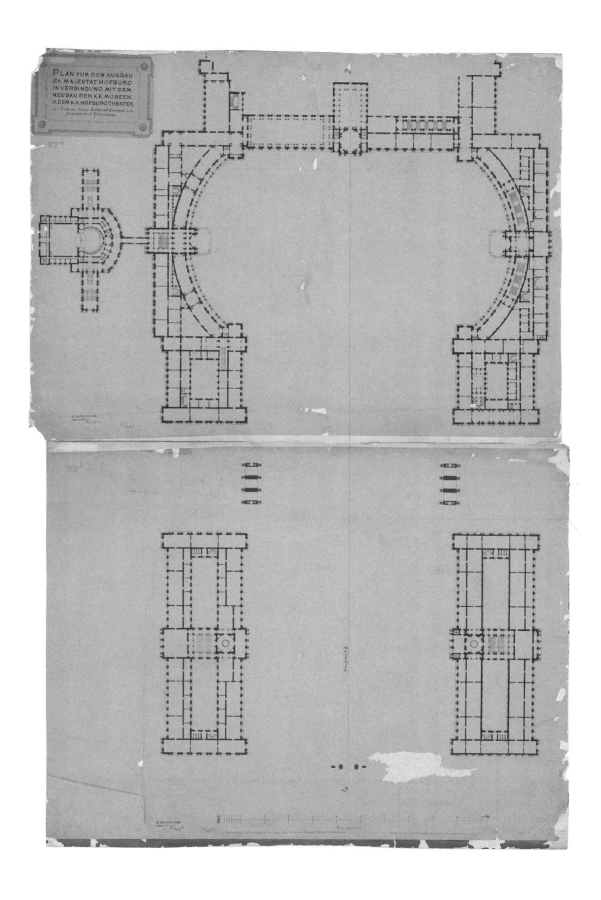

Gottfried Semper,
original plan for the
Imperial Forum, 1869.
ETH Zurich, gta Ar-
chives (© ETH Zurich,
gta Archives).

The Imperial Forum

"Roman architecture of the Imperial period,
the idea of global hegemony expressed in stone,
[contains the seeds of] cosmopolitan architecture of the future [...]"
Gottfried Semper, *Über Baustile*, 1869[28]

In planning a new building for Dresden's art museum in 1837, Semper proposed
embedding the structure within a monumental forum. The plan for enlarging the
city's Zwinger, a unique Baroque ceremonial square, into the "Zwingerforum" was
in the event not executed. Almost half a century later in Vienna the architect was to
take advantage of the opportunity to take up on his ambitious Dresden project,
albeit under different conditions. The style of the Roman Empire represented for
Semper "the synthesis of two apparently contradictory cultural outlooks, namely
that of individual effort and of assimilation into a whole. It marshals many separate
spaces of varying dimensions and orders of importance around a large central area,
according to the principal of co-ordination and subordination, where everything
upholds and supports each other; each individual element is necessary for the
whole, without the latter ceasing either externally or internally to proclaim itself an
individual with appropriate organs and members and the possibility of existing, if
need be, on its own".
The master plan, which came to be known in Vienna as the Kaiserforum, or Imperial Forum, was to integrate the new museums in a larger whole that was oriented
around the Hofburg as the monarchy's centre of power.[29] It was thereby to endow
the image of empire with an architectural focus. Extending as far as the former
imperial stables (today: Museumsquartier), the Imperial Forum was also to form a
counterweight balancing the direction of movement formed by the Ringstrasse. The
original plan foresaw the two museums facing each other on the outer side of the
Ringstrasse and a building fronting the Leopoldine wing of the Hofburg. The
central section of the latter structure was to accommodate a throne room (not
executed). Further, on a line with the museums, buildings of segment form were to

face each other on the inner side of the Ringstrasse (partially realised in the form of the Neue Burg). Other elements were the new Court Theatre (constructed in 1874-88 at a different location opposite the City Hall begun in 1872). Finally, two triumphal arches (not executed) were to span the Ringstrasse linking the areas. Today, the overall plan and inner coherence of the buildings does not appear clearly at first glance, especially because of the lack of the structural element spanning the Ringstrasse. The plan for an arch was scrapped at an early stage, for even at that date the city fathers saw in it an obstruction to growing traffic on Vienna's central ceremonial boulevard. Certainly, it is only with knowledge of the original plan that the museum's façades, which today have a hermetic aspect, appear logical and consistent. With their by no means plain, but in comparison nonetheless more modest architectonic instrumentation, they are subordinate to the expansive and voluminous façade of the Neue Burg, the seat of imperial power.

At the time of planning, the use of the monumental buildings was envisaged as follows: The Burggarten wing (today: Neue Burg) as "the residence of their majesties" was to be equipped with dining rooms, numerous ancillary rooms, audience and working rooms, quarters for the guards, and apartments for officials. The throne room (not executed) was to have a large entry hall on the ground floor and be connected by a "one-armed" ceremonial staircase with the large staircases of the two segment wing tracts (Neue Burg). In the corps de logis (today: the Museum of

Aerial view of the Imperial Forum. City of Vienna, MA41 Stadt-vermessung (© Stadt Wien).

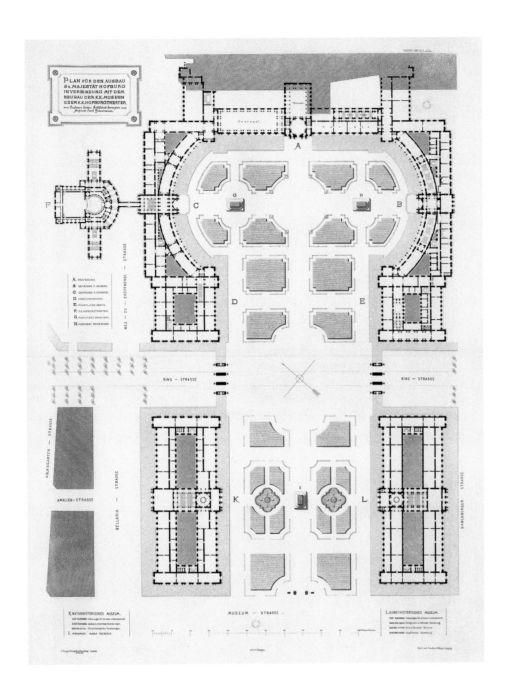

Gottfried Semper and Carl Hasenauer, "Plan für den Ausbau Sr. Majestät Hofburg in Verbindung mit dem Neubau der K. K. Museen und des K. K. Hofburgtheaters", 1871. ETH Zurich, gta Archives (© ETH Zurich, gta Archives).

Ethnology), the arcaded courtyard, as eventually constructed was already planned, around which "larger and smaller ceremonial halls were to be grouped". Located opposite the Neue Burg, the Volksgarten wing, which was never to be built, was intended to serve as guest quarters for "foreign sovereigns and their suites".

A Grand Urban Project Unfinished

By the time Semper had departed the scene only the museums had advanced beyond the planning stage. They were completed in 1891, and together with the Court Theatre represent Hasenauer's major achievements. Construction of the buildings on Heldenplatz commenced based on Semper's plans in 1887. By 1894, the exterior walls of the Burggarten wing (today the Neue Burg) had been completed. Hasenauer passed away the same year. Semper had left Vienna in 1877. From this

Friedrich Ohmann, Imperial Forum, view towards Neue Burg, 1906. Wien Museum, Inv. No. 49.050/4 (© Wien Museum).

time on, work proceeded desultorily based on the existing detailed plans. Various court officials took on responsibility for managing construction. The first alterations to the interior were undertaken, doubtless because of some bewilderment about how such massive expanses of space were to be employed. In 1898, Friedrich Ohmann assumed direction of construction. His contribution to the project was limited to the addition of a glasshouse in the Burggarten. Beyond this, Ohmann was to leave behind but a modest imprint: a number of the rooms on the second floor of the Neue Burg, the entry hall and a large portion of the arcaded courtyard in the corps de logis (Museum of Ethnology). In 1906, Franz Ferdinand, heir to the imperial throne, assumed chairmanship of the Burgbaukommission, or Palace Building Commission. This gave rise to extensive changes, because in Franz Ferdinand's view, "the project by Semper and Hasenauer suffers from several faults. In particular, it fails entirely to take into account the historic value and beauty of the old palace, as can be seen in the planned obstruction of the view of the Leopoldine wing. [...] Finally, the complex is too large for current needs. [...] The main floor of the new palace wing bordering on the Imperial Garden (Neue Burg), up to which 104 steps lead, is because of its height suitable neither as living quarters nor for ceremonial purposes. [...] As to the construction of the wing bordering the Volksgarten, symmetry demands that it face the wing of the palace near the Imperial Garden, and that its principal mass harmonise with that of the building opposite. [...] This building could be intended only for use as a museum."[30]

Friedrich Ohmann was removed from his post in 1907 and replaced by Ludwig Baumann who displayed greater organizational talent. The "well-known master for solving difficult ground plans" adopted his predecessor's last plan from 1906 as his guide.[31] He planned to replicate the corps de logis (Museum of Ethnology) on the opposite side, and so realize only part of the building as originally planned. As a substitute for the section of the building in segment form thus eliminated, Ohmann had proposed a linear and rhythmic row of columns with a pavilion system. Baumann now essentially adopted this motif, but cited yet more clearly Semper's original plan by defining the square in segment form.

The decisive difference to Ohmann's plan lies in the treatment of the historical buildings in the area. Baumann touches neither the façade of the Leopoldine wing of the Imperial Palace nor Louis Montoyer's Festsaal ("Hall of Ceremonies"), of 1804. Ohmann had envisaged carrying out the plan for a throne room wing, as originally provided in the plan by Semper and Hasenauer, which would have obstructed the view of the old Imperial Palace. In so doing, he hastened his demise as palace architect. Franz Ferdinand had made preservation of the historic architectural substance a condition *sine qua non*. Baumann planned for this area only a system of pavilions connected by a colonnade. This solution was to link the building line of the old Imperial Palace, characterised by its restless set-offs, with the forum's central axis and thus provide it with an orderly finish. Finally, for the other end of the forum, he planned a matching element: a colonnade at the centre of which he added a triumphal arch on the axis of the equestrian statues of Prince Eugene and Archduke Karl erected in 1860 and 1865 respectively. It was to define "the end of the garden and [form] the appropriate monumental backdrop for the monument to Maria Theresia".[32]

The general plan was quickly approved. Baumann planned to complete preliminary work by 1911 and start actual construction of the extension in 1912. He hoped to be able to finish the forum by 1917. In 1907, beyond a number of immediate measures, Baumann started to draft plans for the new building for "museum use" opposite the corps de logis. The design for the façade of the "Imperial Royal Museum on the Ringstrasse" shows a building that echoed its "model" in proportions and distribution of mass, as well as in its main horizontal and vertical lines. However, in form and the articulation of surfaces, Baumann's simplification went so far as to schematise. In reducing the classical architectural elements of organisation to their formal framework, Baumann wished to proceed very systematically: an "architecture of windows" was transformed into a more contemporary "architecture of columns". By so doing, Baumann responded to one of the major points of criticism of Semper and Hasenauer's buildings, namely that they failed to allow sufficient light and air inside. The plan was apparently altered again subsequently, because a very detailed model of the 1910 plans (today in the Silver Collection of the Hofburg) reveals a building completely adapted to the corps de logis. This may possibly have been due to the conservative influence of Franz Ferdinand. In March 1908, Baumann reported to the Building Commission that he had completed the plan and that Franz Ferdinand had already indicated his agreement in principle. At the beginning of April however, Emperor Franz Josef issued an edict by which, "construction of the Volksgarten Wing was not to commence; *ad acta!*".[33] Withdrawal of the necessary funding sounded the death-knell for the Volksgarten Wing. In April 1913, Franz Josef reiterated that plans for the building were to be abandoned. The funds of the Urban Extension Fund thus made available were to be used for preservation of Schönbrunn and Belvedere palaces.

The Austrian Republic, established in 1918, was remarkably sluggish in dissolving "His Majesty's Construction Administration". This took place only in 1922 and after the capital of the Urban Extension Fund, which was indispensable for employing the necessary personnel and carrying out larger projects, fell victim to currency devaluation. "Only Hofrat Baumann remained on as artistic advisor to the

Burghauptmannschaft [Imperial Palace Administration]".[31] The latter body had assumed the task of "completing the ceremonial halls to the extent that, together with the historic apartments in the old Imperial Palace, they could be used for important social events such as balls, major conferences, and other representative functions". Starting in 1922 the Burghauptmannschaft raised the capital required to provisionally complete the rooms, which remained in part unfinished. The funds were obtained both through rental fees and the sale of tickets for admission to those of the old palace's state apartments, which had been made accessible to the general public in 1918. "The entire magnificent staircase [is occasionally] occupied by shoe, clothes and fur firms […] garish, ugly advertisements obscure the beautiful marble walls, and a public very different from that for which they were intended populates the halls. Nothing could characterise better the changing times".[35]

Ludwig Baumann, Imperial Forum, colonnades bordering the Volksgarten, 1907. Wien Museum, Baumann bequest (© Wien Museum).

Museum buildings, 1816–1937

1816–1830	Munich, Glyptothek (Leo von Klenze)
1823–1830	Berlin, Altes Museum (Karl Friedrich Schinkel)
1823–1848	London, British Museum (Sir Robert Smirke)
1826–1836	Munich, Alte Pinakothek (Leo von Klenze)
1832–1838	London, National Gallery (William Wilkins)
1837–1846	Karlsruhe, Kunsthalle (Heinrich Hübsch)
1839–1852	St. Petersburg, New Hermitage (Leo von Klenze)
1841–1850	Berlin, Neues Museum (Friedrich August Stüler)
1846–1854	Munich, Neue Pinakothek (Friedrich von Gärtner and August von Voit)
1847–1855	Dresden, Gemäldegalerie (Gottfried Semper)
1850–1866	Stockholm, National Museum (Friedrich August Stüler)
1865–1876	Berlin, Alte Nationalgalerie (Friedrich August Stüler)
1870–1876	Boston, Museum of Fine Arts (John Sturgis and Charles Brigham; after 1907 replaced by a new building at a different location)

1871   **27 November: Construction of Kunsthistorisches Museum begins**

1874–1876   **Construction of scaffolding up to attic story (Wiener Baugesellschaft)**

1874   **Completion of ground floor;**
selection of material and commissions for the interior decoration
(stairs in vestibule, Hall XI of the Collection of Greek and Roman Antiquities, etc.)

1875   **Stone for sculptures in façade spandrels procured**

1877   **Completion of vaults in the Egyptian Collections and Hall XI of the Collection of Greek and Roman Antiquities**

1877–1885	Antwerp, Rijksmuseum (Petrus J. H. Cuypers)

1878   **Installation of first windows**

1879   **Completion of attics and balustrades**

1879 ff.   **Mounting of statues**

1880–1881   **Construction of cupola and tabernacle**

1881 ff.   **Mounting of the statue of Athena (Johannes Benk; execution: k. k. Kunsterzgiesserei) on the cupola; delivery of materials for decoration of the staircase**

1884–1890	Antwerp, Koninklijk Museum voor Schone Kunsten (Jean-Jacques Winders and Frans Van Dijck)

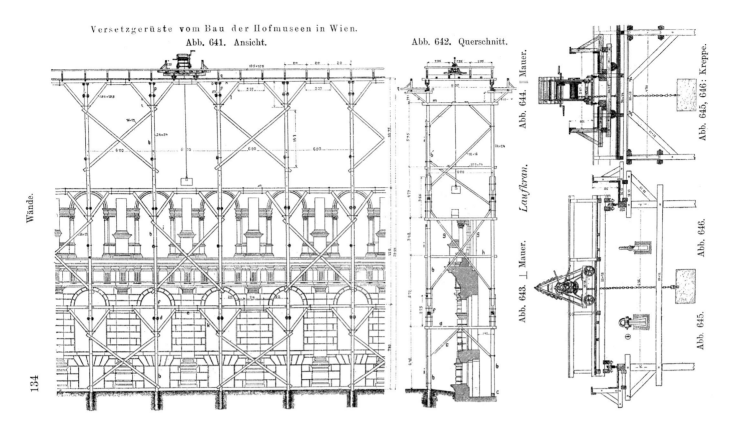

Scaffold for the construction of the imperial museums in Vienna.

1889	**Partial opening of Kunsthistorisches Museum (Collection of Arms and Armour); completion of Egyptian Collections**
1891	**17 October: Kunsthistorisches Museum opens**
1895–1902	New York, Metropolitan Museum of Art, façade unfinished (Richard Morris Hunt)
1897–1904	Berlin, Kaiser Friedrich-Museum (today: Bodemuseum) (Ernst Eberhard von Ihne)
1899–1909	London, Victoria and Albert Museum (Aston Webb)
1910–1930	Berlin, Pergamonmuseum (Alfred Messel and Ludwig Hoffmann)
1911–1913	New York, Metropolitan Museum of Art, north and south wings (McKim, Mead and White)
1937–1941	Washington, National Gallery (John Russell Pope)

The dates cited refer to construction of museum buildings, not the museums' establishment as institutions.

1891 – The Museum Completed

Pages 76–77:
Cartouches bearing the initials of
Emperor Franz Josef I and Empress
Elisabeth in the staircase of Kunst-
historisches Museum.

Maria Theresien-Platz, view
from Museumsplatz towards
Heldenplatz, c. 1935. Wien
Museum, Inv. No. 180.730
(© Wien Museum).

18 October 1891 – Neue Freie Presse

The opening of Kunsthistorisches Museum
Vienna, 17 October

The ceremony at which Kunsthistorisches Museum was opened by the Emperor, and in which all of Vienna's most eminent personalities – both from among official circles, as well as from the arts and sciences – took part, was far more than a festive event. It was a joyous celebration at which the new and youthfully vigorous arts of Vienna celebrated the palace it had designed and decorated for the artworks of past ages, and to which the monarch accorded his fullest acknowledgement and unqualified recognition by his warm praise. At the glittering gathering that filled the museum's rooms were to be found men who had themselves seen all similar works of architecture, which are the pride of other metropolises, and whose judgement must thus be regarded as most competent. All were full of admiration for this work of art, which from now on must be the crown of our city's monumental edifices. The many personalities from abroad who attended the ceremony will be heralds of the new building's magnificence, whose repute can be expected to quickly spread throughout the cultivated world. The builder of the museum, Ober-Baurath Baron Hasenauer, can be certain of the gratitude of every Viennese who hold the city's development and prosperity dear to their hearts. The high praise which the Emperor paid him will be joined in by the entire population, which now will be able to enjoy the art treasures gathered together in the magnificent edifice. High spirits predominated during the tour through the museum which the Emperor undertook accompanied by a numerous suite; indeed the bright sunshine that flooded the halls with light exalted with its radiance this triumph of the Empire's arts. The Emperor's tour lasted approximately two and one half hours. Owing to the extensive tracts to be traversed and bewildering abundance of art objects, the Emperor could stop to admire only the most outstanding and important. The Emperor was exceptionally animated: the beauty and splendour of the building, which owes its existence to his munificence, appeared to make him happier the closer he became acquainted with its details.

In the first department which the Emperor visited, that of the Egyptian Collections, two ancient Egyptian papyrus columns of syenite, which bear the ceilings of both halls, attracted his attention, and he recalled that these had been donated by the Egyptian court architect, Lukovics, a native of Dalmatia, for the construction of the new museum. To curator Dr. von Bergmann he praised the functional arrangement and display of the objects. Among these he remarked upon a particularly massive foot of a statue, which must have been of tremendous dimensions, and enquired whether the fragment might not belong to one of the stone colossi of Memphis. Dr. von Bergmann explained however that there was no evidence of the object's origin.

At the entrance to the Collection of Greek and Roman Antiquities, the Emperor was received by the director, Regierungsrath Dr. Kenner and curator Robert Schneider. He first viewed the collection of Greek vases. In the hall with busts of Roman emperors, the Emperor stood for a long while before the statue of Isis fashioned of black and yellow marble, and observed that this furnished an interesting example of the manner the ancients used colour in the plastic arts. He commented most favourably on the allegorical and mythical scenes of the ceiling and the wall paintings in these halls, which were executed by Professor Eisenmenger, Franz Simm, Professor Karger, Professor Russ, and Ludwig Hans Fischer. In the hall of stone sculpture the Emperor was surprised by the richness and number of treasures exhibited, and admitted that he had no inkling of their extent. He commended the extraordinarily sensitive arrangement which showed each piece to its best advantage, and spent a longer time inspecting the framed miniature portraits on the walls, which Archduke Ferdinand of Tyrol had assembled as a gallery of his most famous contemporaries, and which now for the first time were accessible to the public. The Emperor remarked to Regierungsrath Dr. Kenner that he considered it a matter of great importance that the collections be used intensively for research. In a similar vein, the Emperor had on a previous occasion expressed his views to a delegation concerning the use of an imperial scientific collection, "gentlemen, I use it with pleasure!". In the Collection of Coins and Medals, where curator Domanig explained the display of the objects, the Emperor was particularly interested by the arrangement of the German and Italian coins to provide a chronological illustration of the history of art. In the Department of Old Decorative Arts, which fills not less than nine halls and is under the direction of Regierungsrath Dr. Ilg, the Emperor enquired as to which objects had been transferred from the Imperial Treasury and earlier individual collections, and what artistic and historical considerations informed their being brought together. He first had the famous Burgundian vestments of the Order of Golden Fleece shown and inspected the same closely. In the hall of clocks and astronomical devices a collection of models of various tools from the sixteenth century attracted the Emperor's attention, and he enquired of Regierungsrath Ilg as to their origin. The later replied that the models had been used for the instruction of the children of Archduke Ferdinand of Tyrol. The Emperor spent the longest time in the so-called Golden Hall, and expressed his surprise at the richness of the objects there exhibited. He was particularly delighted by the very extraordinary number of ornamental vessels of rock crystal, topaz, amethyst and other semi-precious stones. In reply to the Emperor's questions, Dr. Ilg confirmed that this was indeed the most important collection of its kind, even in comparison with those of the Louvre and Grünes Gewölbe in Dresden. Examin-

Robert Raschka, *The Opening of Kunsthistorisches Museum by Emperor Franz Josef I on 17 October 1891*. KHM, Gemäldegalerie, Inv. No. 5990.

ing the objects of goldsmiths' art the Emperor remarked that these would no doubt exercise a powerful attraction on the public and draw many visitors to Vienna. Dr. Ilg emphasised in particular the educational value of the objects both for the decorative arts and the public's taste, to which the Emperor nodded in agreement. Before leaving this hall the Emperor walked to its centre, looked all around and praised the beautiful light which prevailed here. In the collection of ivory carvings, the Emperor also expressed his astonishment at the large number of objects. The Emperor strode quickly through the collection of arms and armour accompanied by Dr. Ilg and curator Böheim, as he had viewed this collection when it was first opened. Nonetheless he had shown the tournament and armoury books which are kept here. When the Emperor departed the halls of the ground floor and entered the staircase from the vestibule viewing it from below, he remained still for a moment under the impression of the magnificent architecture and rich painting. He took a few steps back, and clearly most favourably impressed, said, "splendid, lovely!". He then ascended the staircase accompanied by Ober-Baurath Baron Hasenauer who provided information about the painters who had executed the pictures. He spoke very favourably about Makart's paintings in the fanlights. The Emperor liked most particularly the historical frieze by Matsch and Ernst and Gustav Klimt, pupils of the late Laufberger and Professor Berger, and said to the three elated painters, "that must have been an extraordinarily difficult task; I am always delighted when I see your work".

After the Emperor had inspected with great interest the large sculptural compositions by Benk and Weyr in the cupola hall, which honour the patrons of the arts of the House of Habsburg, and expressed his appreciation, he entered the halls of the Picture Gallery, where he was received by Hofrath von Engerth and Vice Director Schäffer. From his remarks it was clear that the Emperor is very well acquainted with the former Belvedere Gallery, for although he walked at a quick pace through the halls, he noted immediately all of the pictures which had been newly added. He was most delighted to find so many new paintings which he himself had never seen. He stayed for a while in the Rubens Hall, about which he had enquired upon entering the galleries, and praised the effect the large paintings now made in the new frames executed according to Baron Hasenauer's designs. He also viewed the portraits by Van Dyck and stated that these vigorous paintings have an unmistakable influence on the best portraitists of our time. He was particularly interested by the characteristic portrait of Archduke Leopold Wilhelm, which is newly exhibited, and the war scenes by Snyders and Vermayen. In all of the halls equipped with skylights the Emperor first looked upwards and repeatedly commended the good illumination and full, serene, and even light that only now permitted all the pictures to be shown to their best advantage. He asked Baron Hasenauer to explain the sculptural decoration of the apophyge of the gallery's ceiling and commented with surprise, "every hall is decorated differently". Tilgner's busts of artists in the niches above the doorways of the gallery's halls elicited the Emperor's lively delight. The Emperor expressed to Hofrath von Eger and Vice Director Schäffer his unqualified appreciation for the installation of the galleries and his satisfaction with the newly arranged collection of watercolours on the second floor.

On the first floor, the Emperor was escorted by Baron Hasenauer to a window, affording a wonderful view out onto the Kahlenberg and the monumental buildings of the new Vienna, City Hall, Parliament, Court Theatre, and University. Enraptured by the lovely view the Emperor stood still and said, "it is singularly beautiful".

After completing the tour through the museum, the Emperor was introduced by Baron Hasenauer in the cupola hall on the first floor to some two hundred artists, industrialists, and craftsmen who had been involved in the building's construction. In a loud, clear voice which could be heard some way off he said, "so these are the gentlemen who laboured on this great and beautiful work", and directed the following words to the group, "I express to you who have worked on this building my fullest appreciation; it is a magnificent achievement. The building is truly exquisite". Then the Emperor proceeded to the line of artists and craftsmen and distinguished most of those presented to him by Baron Hasenauer by addressing a few words to them. So he spoke to Ober-Baurath Eduard Kaiser, who had been master builder of the museum, "you have mastered a difficult task over these past twenty years". To the sculptor Weyr he said, "you have truly created an amazing amount", while to the sculptor Benk he expressed his satisfaction and asked about the work upon which he was presently engaged. The painters Professors Eisenmenger and Karger had the honour of speaking at greater length with the Emperor. To craftsmen such as the outstanding stucco artist Detoma, the carpenter and decorator Sigmund Jaray, and many others too, the Emperor addressed kind words of appreciation. The ornamental painter Adolph Falkenstein – artist of many works in Kunsthistorisches Museum, Court Theatre, Parliament, and the hunting lodge in Lainz, etc., who painted the decorative ceiling above the main staircase, as well as that leading to the second floor, and in many of the ground floor galleries – Alois Hanusch, bronze manufacturer to the Imperial Court, as well as the successor to his business enterprise, Rudolph Ermer, were also presented to the Emperor and distinguished by being addressed by him. As the Emperor escorted by Baron Hasenauer departed the cupola hall to stormy acclamations of "long live the Emperor", and descended the stairs, he turned once again to Hasenauer and expressed his warmest appreciation, saying "I must say a special word of thanks to you. Everything turned out very well. The building is as beautiful as the arrangement functional. The objects can only now be seen to their fullest advantage".

Archdukes Karl Ludwig, Albrecht, Rainer, Wilhelm and Ferdinand, who had also taken part in the tour of the museum, expressed their fullest appreciation and admiration. Archduke Karl Ludwig devoted particular attention to the sculptural decoration of the cupola hall.

All the other personalities who had participated in the tour were equally impressed by the museum's architecture, decoration, and the clear display of the collections. One artist well-known for his quick wit opined with some justification, "now the association for the promotion of tourism in Vienna could do nothing better than name Baron Hasenauer an honorary member, for his creation, the museum, will have a greater effect than all the measures hitherto discussed and resolved upon". Indeed, a paean in praise of the museum's architect and his colleagues was sung by a thousand voices. One of our leading scholars said something which certainly merits bearing in mind: "So rich and beautiful as to enrapture us, this temple of the arts also represents a duty, not only to preserve it in all its magnificence, but also to maintain and cultivate further the spirit which gave birth to it, for no sacrifice for the arts and sciences can be too great, and the recognition and appreciation which inspires all of us, shall also be paid in future to all those who thus illustrate the *utile dulci*.

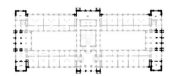

The Façades

The Sculptural Programme

168 m lang | 74 m tief | 25 bis 27 m hoch | 10.778 m² bebaute Fläche
Höhe bis zur Kuppel: 64 m.

The main façade is lent a pronounced vertical accent by the interposed central structure with its cupola, which is subtly echoed by the two corner risalits. Elements articulating the façade are distributed evenly over the entire building. The elevation of the façade is composed in approximately equal measure of a base zone of rough-hewn stone and giant Tuscan pillars, and an upper zone having three-quarter Ionic columns. Rectangular windows in the basement level, and round arch windows in the ground floor are distributed evenly in the base zone. A triglyph frieze and console cornice define the beginning of the first floor with its Ionic Serlian windows. A narrow meander frieze runs along the border of the attic storey, which is provided with rectangular windows. The frieze in the architrave area is decorated alternately with the Austrian Imperial Crown and monogram "F[ranz] J[osef]". A balustrade completes the façade. On the median risalit, free-standing columns positioned on the axis of the lanterns that flank the cupola both create a more plastic appearance and heighten the expressiveness of the structure in the entry area. The architectural idiom of the entire building relies on a variety of High Renaissance forms. The origins of the stylistic orientation selected for the museum can be traced to Klenze's Alte Pinakothek (1836); these had displaced the previously prevailing Classicist tendencies. The sculptural programme harks back to the plan completed by Semper in 1874 for the building's decoration. In the architect's view, the "exterior decoration of an art museum [...] must reflect its contents".[36] It reflects the basic artistic parameters of Semper's theoretical writings and other sources, and is a "representation of the conditions that determine a work of art". A "style" develops at the point that an artwork corresponds "with the history of its development". Semper categorises the "external preconditions" of (artistic) form, simplifying them for this particular purpose, into three categories.

Façade facing Museumsplatz, detail.

Median risalit on Maria Theresien-Platz, main entrance.

On the ground floor, which is primarily to "house objects of applied art" and "the treasures of ancient and more modern craftsmanship", "symbolic allusions to the technical element in the arts are appropriate". Hence the various crafts (the "material") appear here. The "masterpieces of painting and copper engraving" on the first floor are the "most brilliant reflection of the social, political, and religious conditions of the countries and ages to which they belong". Hence, in selecting the motifs one may "take into consideration the influence of the environment on the arts and, conversely, the civilising force of the arts". Allegories of the most important European art centres represent here the "history of art". The statues of the balustrade – "the personal aspect" – manifest the "personal influence of the artist on the direction of his art". In this connection, the artists' balustrade of the Munich Pinakothek may be recalled. Beside the "images of the masters who excelled through the power and originality of their genius and opened new paths" were to be placed those of "a number of poets and men of science, whose inspiring and instructive call fertilised the blossoming of the arts". Following this scheme, the façade on the Babenbergerstrasse side of the museum was to be dedicated to the Ancient World, that on Museumsplatz to Byzantine, Carolingian and Early Medieval art, the façade facing Maria Theresien-Platz to the Renaissance, and finally the Burgring front to modern art.

Façade facing Museumsplatz, detail.

Overleaf: Façade facing Museumsplatz; detail of the attic area of median risalit on Maria Theresien-Platz ("Victory" and arms of Habsburg-Lorraine).

Façade facing Museumsplatz, detail with balustrade figures.

"Art of Antiquity"

Babenbergerstrasse, corner risalit, right[37]

Polygnotus of Thasos (K. Rippel)

Bularchos (Vinzenz Pilz)

Canachus of Sicyon (K. Rippel)

Theodoros of Samos (K. Rippel)

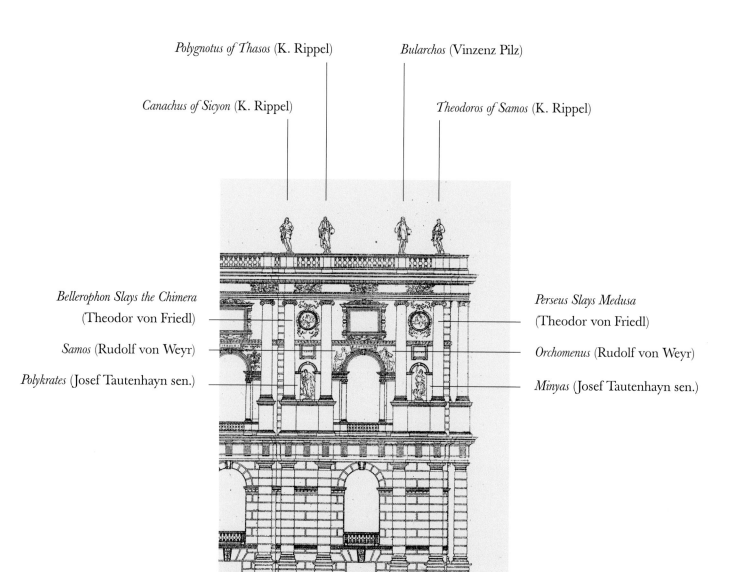

Bellerophon Slays the Chimera (Theodor von Friedl)

Samos (Rudolf von Weyr)

Polykrates (Josef Tautenhayn sen.)

Perseus Slays Medusa (Theodor von Friedl)

Orchomenus (Rudolf von Weyr)

Minyas (Josef Tautenhayn sen.)

Gottfried Semper, "Studie für das Eckrisalit".
Manfred Semper, *Hasenauer und Semper*, Hamburg,
1895, sheet 3 (adaptation).

"Art of Antiquity"

Babenbergerstrasse, median risalit

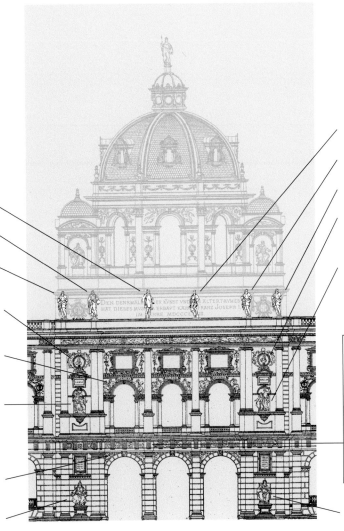

Aristotle (Vinzenz Pilz)

Scopas (Vinzenz Pilz)

Praxiteles (Vinzenz Pilz)

Pygmalion and Aphrodite
(Theodor von Friedl)

*Corinth, Sicyon, Thebes, Athens, Rhodes,
Miletus* (Rudolf von Weyr)

Pericles (Vinzenz Pilz)

*Oread, Dryad, Naiad, Nereid, Sylphid,
Boread* (Rudolf von Weyr)

Applied Arts (Carl Kundmann)

Pythagoras (Vinzenz Pilz)

Polykleitos (Franz Koch)

Phidias (Franz Koch)

Prometheus and Athena
(Theodor von Friedl)

Peisistratos (Vinzenz Pilz)

Metopes:
Dibutades of Corinth (potter's
wheel), *Rhoecus* (bronze
casting), *Clearchos* (hammered
metalwork), *Glaucus* (forging
and welding), *Daedalus of
Athens* (wood sculpture), *Melas
of Chios* (marble sculpture)
(Carl Kundmann)

Architecture (Carl Kundmann)

Gottfried Semper and Carl Hasenauer, museum
façade, final plan. Manfred Semper, *Hasenauer
und Semper,* Hamburg, 1895, sheet 2 (detail,
adaptation).

"Art of Antiquity"

Babenbergerstrasse, corner risalit, left

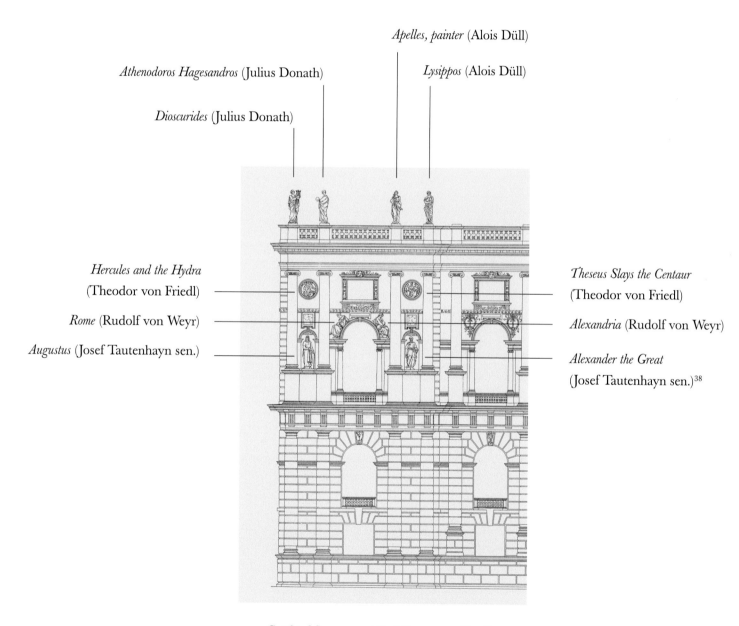

Apelles, painter (Alois Düll)

Athenodoros Hagesandros (Julius Donath)

Lysippos (Alois Düll)

Dioscurides (Julius Donath)

Hercules and the Hydra
(Theodor von Friedl)

Theseus Slays the Centaur
(Theodor von Friedl)

Rome (Rudolf von Weyr)

Alexandria (Rudolf von Weyr)

Augustus (Josef Tautenhayn sen.)

Alexander the Great
(Josef Tautenhayn sen.)[38]

Gottfried Semper and Carl Hasenauer, "Studie
für das Eckrisalit". Manfred Semper, *Hasenauer
und Semper,* Hamburg, 1895, sheet 3 (adaptation).

"Byzantine, Romanesque and Gothic Art"

Museumsplatz, central section

Bernward of Hildesheim (Josef Messner)   *Alcuin* (A. Schwenzer)

William of Sens (Alois Dorn)   *St. Eligius* (Ludwig Simek)

Erwin von Steinbach (Rudolf Zafouk)   *Isidore of Miletus* (Ludwig Simek)

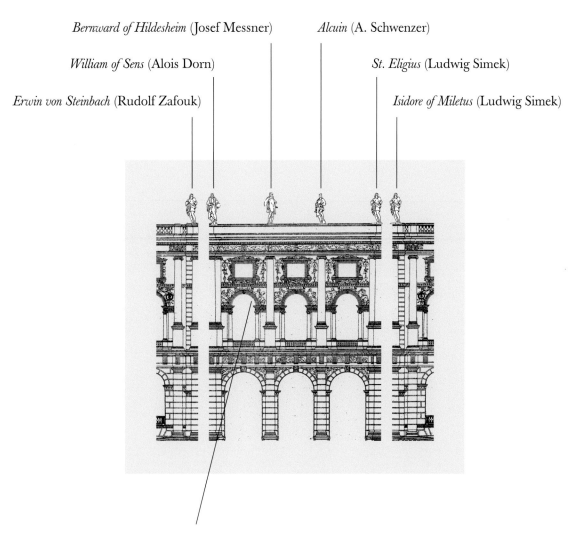

Cologne, Prague, Goslar, Aachen, Ravenna and Byzantium (Constantinople) (Rudolf von Weyr)

Gottfried Semper and Carl Hasenauer, museum façade, final plan. Manfred Semper, *Hasenauer und Semper,* Hamburg, 1895, sheet 2 (detail, adaptation).

Overleaf, double page: Façade facing Museumsplatz.

"Renaissance"

Maria Theresien-Platz, corner risalit, right

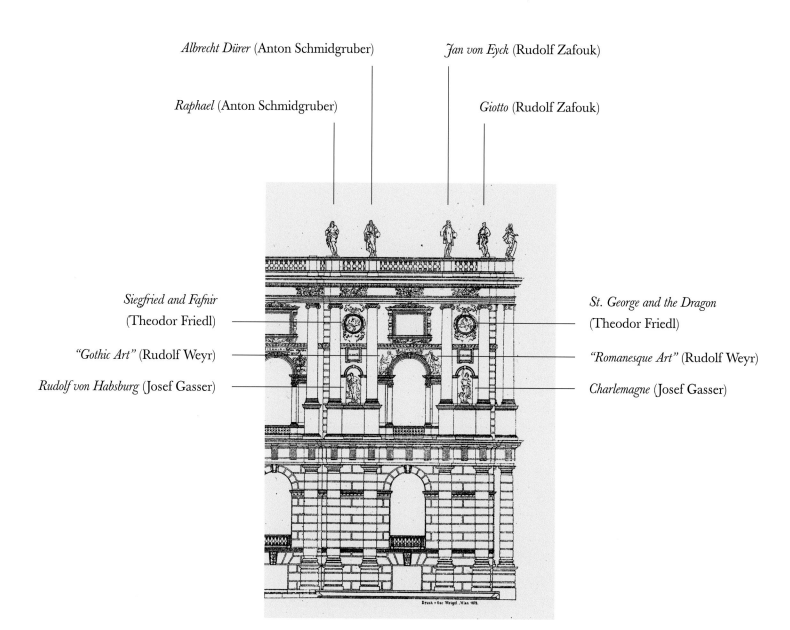

Albrecht Dürer (Anton Schmidgruber)

Jan von Eyck (Rudolf Zafouk)

Raphael (Anton Schmidgruber)

Giotto (Rudolf Zafouk)

Siegfried and Fafnir (Theodor Friedl)

St. George and the Dragon (Theodor Friedl)

"Gothic Art" (Rudolf Weyr)

"Romanesque Art" (Rudolf Weyr)

Rudolf von Habsburg (Josef Gasser)

Charlemagne (Josef Gasser)

Gottfried Semper, "Studie für das Eckrisalit".
Manfred Semper, *Hasenauer und Semper,* Hamburg,
1895, sheet 3 (adaptation).

"Renaissance"

Maria Theresien-Platz, median risalit

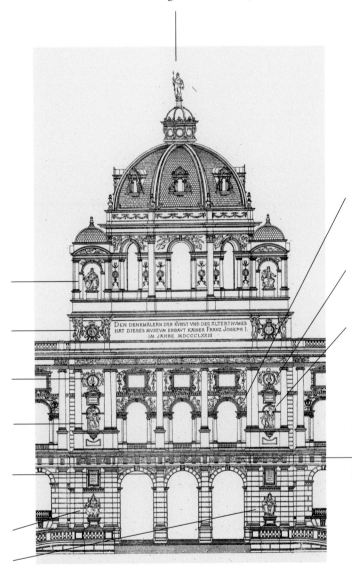

Pallas Athena (Johannes Benk)

Talent, Determination, Passion and
Moderation (Franz Gastell)

Victories (Johannes Benk)

*Giovanni de' Medici as Pope
Leo X* (Victor Tilgner)

Faust and Helena (Ernst Hellmer)

*David, Samuel, Ezekiel, Persian,
Delphic and Cumaean Sibyls*
(Rudolf von Weyr)

Painting (Ernst Helmer)

Sculpture (Johannes Benk)

*Venice, Pisa, Rome, Florence,
Nuremberg and Augsburg*
(Rudolf Weyr)

Lorenzo de' Medici
(Victor Tilgner)

Eros and Psyche (Johannes Benk)

Metopes:

Theophilus Presbyter – enamelwork
and glass painting,
St. Eligius – goldsmithery,
Leo Ostiensis – mosaics, *Bishop
Bernward of Hildesheim* – bronze
casting, *Giacomo Tagliacarne* – gem
engraving, *Jan van Eyck* – oil
painting (Carl Kundmann)

Gottfried Semper and Carl Hasenauer,
museum façade, final plan. Manfred Semper,
Hasenauer und Semper, Hamburg, 1895, sheet 2,
1871.

Sculpture

Eros and Psyche

Samuel and Ezekiel

Allegories of cities: Pisa, Rome, Florence und Nuremberg.

Metopes:
Jan van Eyck and Giacomo Tagliacarne, Bernward von
Hildesheim and Leo von Ostia, Eligius and Theophilus.

Overleaf, double page:
Detail of portal area of median risalit on Maria Theresien-Platz (Ezekiel, Persian Sibyl; Metopes: Bernward
von Hildesheim and Leo von Ostia).

"Renaissance"

Maria Theresien-Platz, corner risalit, left

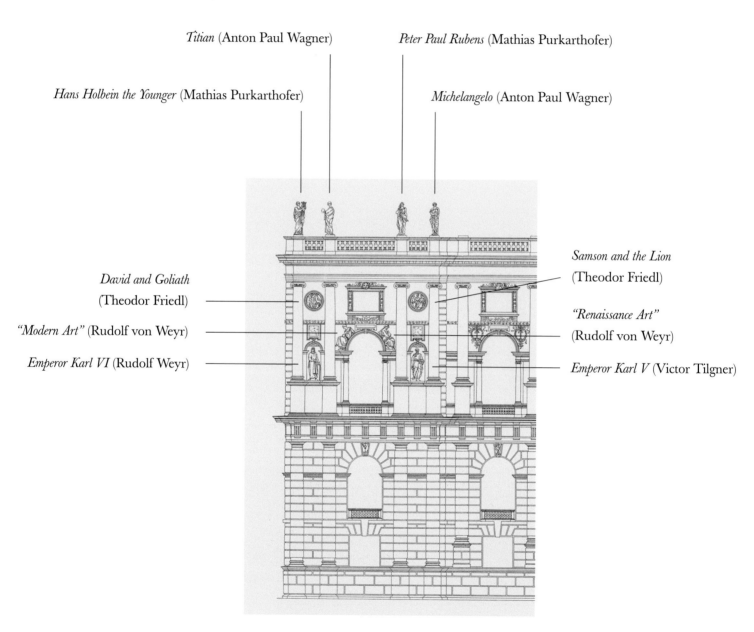

Titian (Anton Paul Wagner)

Peter Paul Rubens (Mathias Purkarthofer)

Hans Holbein the Younger (Mathias Purkarthofer)

Michelangelo (Anton Paul Wagner)

Samson and the Lion (Theodor Friedl)

David and Goliath (Theodor Friedl)

"Modern Art" (Rudolf von Weyr)

"Renaissance Art" (Rudolf von Weyr)

Emperor Karl VI (Rudolf Weyr)

Emperor Karl V (Victor Tilgner)

Gottfried Semper, "Studie für das Eckrisalit".
Manfred Semper, *Hasenauer und Semper*,
Hamburg, 1895, sheet 3 (adaptation).

"Modern Art"

Burgring, centre segment

Peter Cornelius (Victor Tilgner)

Christian Daniel Rauch (Victor Tilgner)

Joseph Ritter von Führich (Victor Tilgner)

Antonio Canova (Franz Pönninger)

Moritz Ludwig von Schwind (Victor Tilgner)

Georg Raphael Donner (Franz Pönninger)

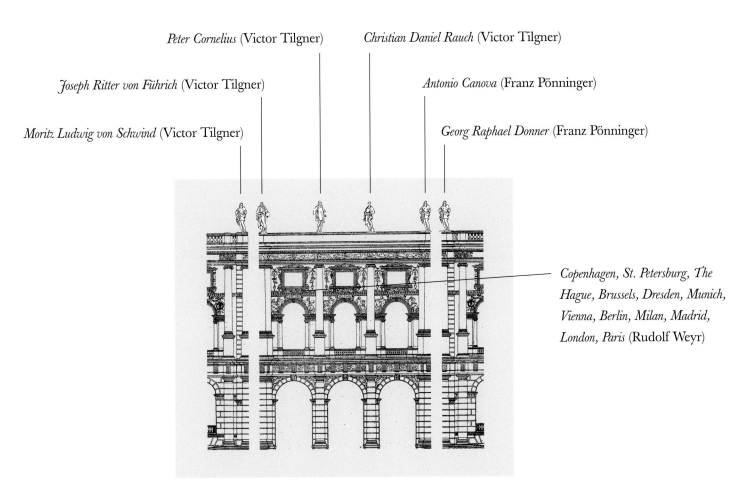

Copenhagen, St. Petersburg, The Hague, Brussels, Dresden, Munich, Vienna, Berlin, Milan, Madrid, London, Paris (Rudolf Weyr)

Museum façade, final plan. Manfred Semper, *Hasenauer und Semper,* Hamburg, 1898, sheet 2 (detail, adaptation).

The selection of personalities representing "Modern Art" for the balustrade was not made by Semper. He referred to "subsequent agreements", but proposed representations of Winckelmann and Lessing as "the greatest modern experts and writers on the arts".[39]

Roof landscape, in the foreground, statue of Albrecht Dürer.

Figures on the balustrade, façade facing Babenbergerstrasse (left to right: Aristotle,
Pythagoras, Polykleitos).

Detail of attic, median risalit on
Maria Theresien-Platz (Victoria).

Roof landscape: lanterns.

Following double pages:
Figures on the balustrade, façade facing Babenbergerstrasse (left to right: Theodoros of Samos, Bularchos, Polygnotus of Thasos, Canachus of Sicyon).
View towards the historic centre of Vienna. In the foreground, one of Johannes Benk's figures of "Victory"; visible in the background, the Minoritenkirche.
Sgraffito decoration, interior courtyard façades. Ferdinand Julius Laufberger created thirty-eight personifications of the arts and trades.

PHIDIAS
APELLES

Interior
Vestibule, Staircase and Cupola Hall

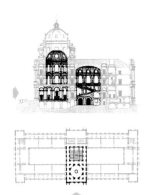

"The most sublime of which Vienna's highly developed architecture, decorative arts and applied arts are capable has been mobilised here to glorify and exalt with figural and ornamental adornment the museum's interior down to the smallest detail. The building which is to serve as a frame for the most supreme of the arts must itself be an artwork of the highest order".
(Carl von Lützow)[40]

The museum's vestibule, staircase and cupola hall form a dramatic unity which together create an appropriately impressive stage for the achievements of the arts, the museum's builder, Franz Josef I, and his predecessors. With the new Munich Pinakothek (1836), the museum as an institution was definitively freed from its architectural union with a princely residence. It is remarkable, however, that the feudal iconography of earlier galleries, for example, the Louvre's Salle Rotonde as a Napoleonic hall of fame, was very largely maintained in the newly created decorative cycles. The formally decorated Stiftersaal, or "Founder's Hall", in the upper vestibule of the Munich Pinakothek contains a frieze of reliefs depicting the history of Bavaria with full-length portraits of its rulers (rededicated 1910, destroyed 1945). In Klenze's buildings, the richness of decoration and colour reaches its apex in the galleries themselves however.[41] The entrance hall and staircase were used in a restrained manner. Similarly, in the Dresden Gemäldegalerie (1847–54), Semper employed a gradual intensification of the means of expression. In Vienna, this deliberate prelude, the purposely staged ascent, is at once abbreviated and reaches its culmination in the mammoth staircase and cupola hall, which in respect of its decorative programme can most certainly be considered a "successor" to the Stiftersaal in the Munich Pinakothek.

Vestibule with a view
onto the staircase and
through the oculus to
the cupola hall.

Vestibule

In the vestibule, a vault with an oculus, or round aperture, rises above the floor decorated with black and white intarsia. This aperture in the vault affords a first view of the cupola hall above. The allusion to the oculus of the dome of the Pantheon in Rome, which however is open to the sky, is a reference to architectural history. As an "amuse-gueule" it affords a preview of what is to follow and conforms to the "progressive heightening of effects from entrance to interior of the main floor" championed by Semper.[42] The restrained decorative programme of the vestibule arch evinces the preference for the Renaissance, which dominates the main façade. The portraits of Bramante, Michelangelo, Raphael and Benvenuto Cellini (Victor Tilgner) with their corresponding inscriptions complement the overall monochromatic appearance. To the right and left of the vestibule's central axis that leads to the staircase, of steps and aedicula portals lead the visitor to the galleries located on the ground floor above. Emerging from the semidarkness of the vestibule, the principal path of access ascends finally over the staircase, which in the most favourable conditions is flooded by sunlight, to the cupola hall, the highpoint of imperial representation. In the decoration and configuration of the staircase Semper and Hasenauer in important respects adopted as model the Late Baroque palace at Caserta near Naples. The royal palace was built starting in 1752 based on plans by Luigi Vanvitelli who was inspired by Versailles. The building is one of the most outstanding examples of European palace architecture. The palace was completed by the Bourbons shortly after the end of Habsburg rule in Naples, thus lending what could be said to be a somewhat piquant note to the direct reference made to it in the architecture of Kunsthistorisches Museum.

Canova's sculpture *Theseus and the Centaur* on the staircase landing signals another emphatic highpoint in the staging of the room. The story of the creation of this monumental sculpture provided good justification for its transfer from the Theseus Temple in the Volksgarten, and display in a prominent location in the new museum: The sculpture was originally planned for Napoleon. Following the French emperor's

Staircase ca. 1910. Wien Museum, Inv. No. 79.000/8759 (© Wien Museum).

Our Vienna correspondent telegraphs: "I mentioned some time ago that Canova's famous marble group of Theseus and the Centaur was being transported from the Greek Temple, erected over it in the Volksgarten of that city, to the Museum of Art on the other side of the Ring. The Centaur was transposed without difficulty and is already on the pedestal which fills the recess of the first landing on the magnificent staircase of the museum. Yesterday the Theseus was laid upon one of the low heavy carts built expressly for the transport of weighty objects, and was drawn through the gardens toward the gate. The cart had to pass over one of the water drains which run under the Volksgarten. The weight was too much for the thin vault, which gave way, and suddenly the cart sank on one side, turned over, and the statue lay shattered on the ground. The right arm which holds the club on high was broken off at the shoulder. The statue was raised and placed under the trees of the Volksgarten, whither," adds our correspondent, the whole city will run to see it when the news of the mishap gets afloat."

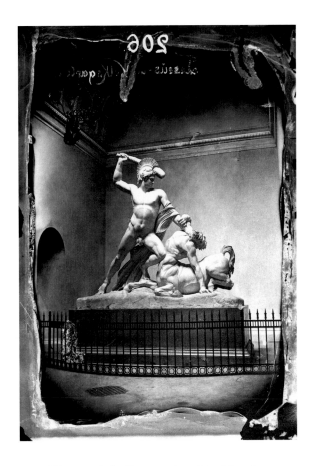

Report by the London correspondent of the *New York Times* about the transport of *Theseus and the Centaur* from the Theseus Temple in Volksgarten to the new museum. *The New York Times*, 16 November, 1890 (© The New York Times).

Theseus and the Centaur at its original location. Vienna, Österreichische Nationalbibliothek, Picture Archive, Inv. No. WB 142 c (© Österreichische Nationalbibliothek).

Peter von Nobile, Theseus Temple in Vienna's Volksgarten, built 1819–23. The original site of Canova's *Theseus and the Centaur*, the temple is a small-scale reproduction of the Theseion in Athens.

Staircase in the late Baroque Palazzo Reale in Caserta near Naples. Constructed in 1752 according to plans by
Luigi Vanvitelli.

final defeat however, the Classicist work was executed in 1819 for Franz I and
brought to Vienna.[43]

Upon reaching the landing, visitors find their attention directed to the cupola hall,
the sacrally charged finale to the architectural orchestration. After the virtually
monochromatic decoration of the vestibule, here at the circular arcade at the top of
the staircase, magnificent coloration and an opulence of forms and images unfold,
obscuring the architectural skeleton. The walls perforated by apertures create
multiple visual relationships which characterise the entire central axis of the building. All the more strikingly then does the ceiling painting, hermetically set off in a
massive frame, contrast with the open space suffused with light. In this manner the
viewer's eye is impelled to the cupola hall.

Following double pages:
Vestibule ceiling with busts of Cellini, Raphael, Michelangelo and Bramante.

Vestibule floor made of Carrara II marble and black Belgian limestone.

Staircase, view towards cupola hall.

Kunsthistorisches Museum: staircase, view towards cupola hall.

Vestibule, view towards staircase.

Staircase: The Decorative Programme

Hans Makart (1840–84) had originally been commissioned to execute the painting for the ceiling as well as fanlight, spandrel, and intercolumnar areas. The contract was signed in February 1881; in the same year an imperial delegation was able to view the artist's initial sketches. Makart first completed the fanlight paintings depicting "classical heroes of painting" and their "favourite materials".[44] He also produced designs for the spandrel pictures and the planned ceiling painting, *Triumph of Darkness over Light.* Makart's early death, however, also spelt the end of the original plan for a uniform style of decoration. Half a year later, Hans Canon (1829–85), a student of Waldmüller, received the commission for the ceiling painting. At the time, the artist was occupied with the decoration of Naturhistorisches Museum. Canon however died before he was able to execute the sketches which he had based on Makart's initial work. Finally, in 1887, Mihály Munkácsy (1844–1900), a Hungarian artist who was part of the Parisian art scene, was given the commission. The monumental oil painting, *Apotheosis of the Renaissance,* which was completed in a specially rented atelier, was shipped to Vienna in 1890 to be mounted.

In 1890, six years after Makart's death, Franz Matsch (1861–1942), Ernst Klimt (1864–92), and Gustav Klimt (1862–1918) were commissioned to paint the spandrel pictures. The young painters had already provided a sample of their work in the Hermes Villa. Encouraged by their mentor, Eitelberger, they had joined together in 1883 to form the Künstler-Companie.[45] Starting in 1886 they worked together with Hasenauer on a more ambitious project, the Burgtheater, which was then under construction. In the judgement of their contemporary, Ilg, this "clover leaf of artists" which had emerged from the Vienna School of Decorative Arts followed in the footsteps of the "Makart's genius, whose festive decorative approach, abundance of figures and colouristic magnificence, none of Vienna's artists [understood] better" than they.[46] From today's vantage point however, the quality that clearly distinguishes their work from Makart's vivid Neo-Baroque richness of figures and sometimes explicitly open painting technique is to be found in the style of Julius Berger.

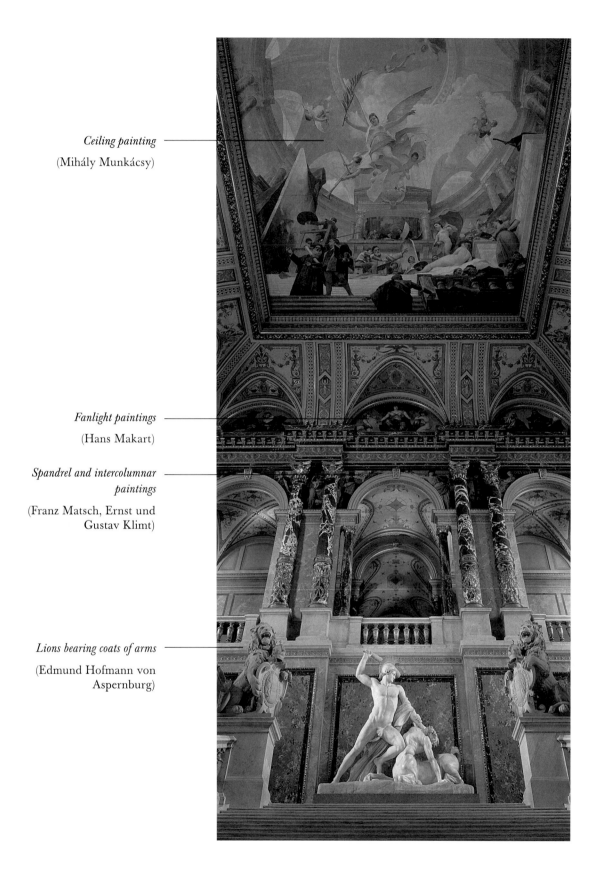

Ceiling painting
(Mihály Munkácsy)

Fanlight paintings
(Hans Makart)

Spandrel and intercolumnar paintings

(Franz Matsch, Ernst und Gustav Klimt)

Lions bearing coats of arms

(Edmund Hofmann von Aspernburg)

Berger was one of the group's instructors at the School of Decorative Arts from 1881, and his style was characterised by flatter, more restrained and dry forms. Despite the obvious admiration for the late Makart as expressed by Ilg in the text quoted above, the youthful successors were allowed to deviate from the original concept. For the spandrels this had foreseen simple allegories reflecting the subject of the fanlight pictures. "If Munkácsy's ceiling is to portray the ideal apotheosis of art, and Makart's fanlight pictures the classical heroes of painting with their favourite materials, so our cycle [i.e. spandrel and intercolumnar paintings] expands on this idea, and adds to the areas of painting other directions that are open to the visual arts". Ilg also desired that the artists make reference to the contents of the imperial collections, if possible depicting some of their objects as faithfully as possible. The programme of the paintings for spandrels and intercolumnar areas was not however to be "too pedantic or strictly instructive", but highlight "in an entirely free artistic" manner "individual, mainly characteristic" objects. The viewer thus should not expect "strict historical completeness". As these pictures were "rigorously set off from Makart's fanlights by the elements of the monumental architecture […] the cycle was to be viewed on its own".[47]

For the genre portrayals of the "classical heroes of painting" the Munich Pinakothek again served as model. In the fanlight areas of the loggias in front of the galleries, Peter Cornelius (who is immortalised on the balustrade of Kunsthistorisches Museum facing Burgring) had realised a comparable, albeit more complex concept.

Fanlight Paintings

The staging of the "classical heroes of painting" is at once appealing to the senses and playful. The same approach is also evident in spandrel and intercolumnar areas. The protagonists appear accompanied by the objects of their work come to life. These favoured subjects are disengaged from the historical context of their creation and used in free association. By systematically employing gold tones, Makart, Klimt and Matsch created a harmonious colour relationship between fanlight, spandrel pictures, and decorative elements of the surrounding architecture, for example, column capitals..

Hans Holbein the Younger

1497–1543. Makart made use here in a suggestive manner of the portrait of Jane Seymour, King Henry VIII's third wife (KHM, Gemäldegalerie, Inv. No. 881) as well as what was formerly believed to be a self-portrait of the artist (*Portrait of a Man with a Red Cap*, 1532/33; Basel, Kunstmuseum).

Allegory of the Law and Truth of Representation

The powerful allegorical figure holds out in her left hand a statuette of Nike (Roman: Victoria), the goddess of victory. With her right hand she points a stylus to an as yet blank canvas that is held by a youthful genius, whilst a matching figure opposite leans upon a reflecting shield. He who is victorious is interpreted thus as he who creates a "true" likeness.

Albrecht Dürer

1471–1528. Makart used Dürer's *Self-Portrait in a Fur Coat* (1500; Munich, Alte Pinakothek), so as to depict the artist in an authentic manner in the small scene. In posture and body language the female figure was inspired by Dürer's engraving *Melencolia I* (1514).

Raphael

1483–1530. Based on the self-portrait in Florence (Uffizi Galleries) Raphael appears here in the company of a model who is a reference to the *Loreto Madonna* (1511/12; Chantilly, Musée Condé). For this painting Makart did not use the *Madonna in the Meadow* (c. 1505/06; Inv. No. 175) and thus does not make explicit reference to the imperial collections.

Hans Makart, Hans Holbein the Elder

Hans Makart, *Allegory of the Law and Truth of Representation.*

Hans Makart, Albrecht Dürer

Hans Makart, Raphael

Rembrandt Harmenszoon van Rijn

1606–69. For this painting Makart decided in favour of a restrained treatment: two muscular nudes hold a portrait medallion. The depiction echoes a type of Rembrandt's self-portraits prominently represented in the imperial collections in the form of the *Large Self-Portrait* (1652; Inv. No. 411).

Peter Paul Rubens

1577–1640. The relationship between painter and model – Makart here cites Rubens' portrait of his second wife, Helena Fourment (*The Fur,* c. 1636/38; KHM, Gemäldegalerie, Inv. No. 688) – is reflected in the intimate embrace of the two, although the dynamism and initiative is reserved to the "painter prince". For this painting too, Makart did not make use of the self-portrait in the museum's collections (c. 1638/40; KHM, Gemäldegalerie, Inv. No. 527), which was painted at about the same time as *The Fur*, but instead referred to an earlier work dating to 1623/24 (Windsor Castle, Royal Collection).

Michelangelo Buonarroti

1475–1564. Michelangelo's Adam (Vatican, ceiling fresco, Sistine Chapel, *Creation of Adam,* 1508–12) appears viewed from the rear leaning on an Ionic column against a red cloth backdrop. He is observed by the artist engaged in the process of creation, who thus assumes the place of the Almighty.

Allegory of Religious and Profane Painting

As a symbol of all-embracing triumph the allegorical figure holds a palm branch in her outstretched arms, whilst Fama's trumpet, which has performed its task of spreading fame (also rumour), now lies unused at her feet. Representative of religious painting are on the left, Raphael's *Sistine Madonna* (c. 1512/13; Dresden, Gemäldegalerie Alte Meister), for profane painting on the right, the artist's Galatea (*Triumph of Galatea,* c. 1511/15; Rome, Villa Farnesina).

Hans Makart, Rembrandt Harmenszoon van Rijn

Hans Makart, Peter Paul Rubens

Hans Makart, Michelangelo Buonarroti

Hans Makart, Allegory of Religious and
Profane Painting

Titian

Around 1488–1576. The nude female figure reclining on a bed and the portrait are two themes typical of Titian, from the early *Sleeping Venus* (around 1508/10; Dresden, Gemäldegalerie Alte Meister), which was executed together with Giorgione, to the famed Venus of Urbino (1538; Florence Uffizi Galleries) to the diverse variants, *Danae* (c. 1560/65; KHM, Gemäldegalerie, Inv. No. 90), *Venus with the Organ Player* (c. 1550; Madrid, Museo del Prado), or the *Venus with the Lute Player* (c. 1560; New York, The Metropolitan Museum of Art). Makart's paraphrase refers in particular to the two last named paintings by Titian: The artist's effigy was inspired by two late self-portraits (c. 1546/47 [?]; Berlin, Staatliche Museen, Gemäldegalerie, and c. 1562; Madrid, Museo del Prado).

Anthony van Dyck

1599–1641. The hitherto accepted identification of the portrait as Bartolomé Esteban Murillo (1618–82) may be subject to question. In Makart's sketch this fanlight is designated as "Antonius van Dyck". Indeed, the "model" displays greater similarities with van Dyck's various depictions of the Lamentation of Christ than with the work of the Spanish artist.

Diego Velázquez

1599–1660. Like Rembrandt in the fanlight opposite, Velázquez is portrayed in a medallion, thus forming a compositional pendant to the former. Makart drew his inspiration from Velázquez's self-portrait (1643) in the Uffizi in Florence.

Leonardo da Vinci

145–1519. Melancholic and visibly exhausted, the model lies before the artist. The model has but a distant relation to Leonardo's work and for compositional reasons echoes the portrayal of Titian. The depiction of Leonardo relies on his Turin self-portrait (drawing in sanguine, c. 1512; Turin, Biblioteca Reale).

Hans Makart, Titian

Hans Makart, Anthony van Dyck (?)

Hans Makart, Diego Velázquez

Hans Makart, Leonardo da Vinci

Spandrel and Intercolumnar Paintings

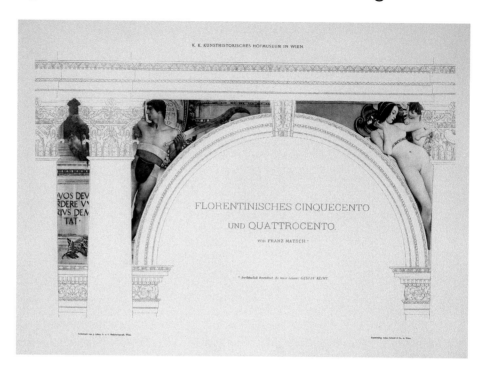

Gustav Klimt, "Florentinisches Cinquecento und Quattrocento", in: Albert Ilg, *Zwickelbilder im Stiegenhause des k. k. Kunsthistorischen Hof-Museums zu Wien von Ernst und Gustav Klimt und Franz Matsch,* table XI, Vienna, 1893.

"Egypt"[48]

A female nude stands before an ornamental background, which combines architectural motives, hieroglyphics, images of the gods Horus and Thoth, and the goddess Nekhbet's vulture. Klimt deviated conspicuously from Egyptian convention, which with but few exceptions portrays only children or prisoners in the nude. In her right hand the female figure holds an ankh, which was also used in Egyptian hieroglyphics as the symbol of life.

Between the columns on the right, i.e. in the "intercolumnar" area, Klimt depicts an uschabti box, statues of Isis and Ptah, who was the principal divinity of Memphis, a scribe, a wooden sarcophagus cover, and in the background, the capital of a Hathor column. None of these were based on objects from the imperial collections. Klimt integrates the animated female figure into the background and also cites her facial features in the sarcophagus cover, thus unifying different levels of reality with compositional virtuosity. This approach is followed throughout the spandrel and intercolumnar paintings in the staircase.

Gustav Klimt, "Egypt"

Gustav Klimt, "Old Italian Art"

■ "Old Italian Art"

In this painting Klimt focuses on the two figures, placing less emphasis on the artworks. A young man attired in the Florentine manner of the fifteenth century pauses from his reading and observes the female figure opposite who is surrounded by a magnificent halo. Her gaze is cast on a putto with halo, wings, and shield. Above, a bronze bust of Dante is to be seen. The figures are accompanied by a frieze of floral garlands and angels' heads based on the work of the Florentine Luca della Robbia (c. 1400–82).

"The German Renaissance"

The characteristic head of Emperor Rudolph II (1552-1612), in Albert Ilg's words, "the greatest art lover of the Habsburg dynasty", together with the inscription dominates the composition. Klimt's model was the bronze bust by the sculptor to the imperial court, Adriaen de Vries (1607; KHM, Kunstkammer, Inv. No. 5491). Dressed in costumes which are documented, for example, in portraits by Hans Holbein the Younger (1497/98-1543), the figures lean in a relaxed and casual fashion against the edge of the spandrels. The young woman examines a coconut goblet, similar to that created in Augsburg around 1570, which is to be found in the Kunstkammer (Inv. No. KK 919). The dignified old man in court costume grasps a closed book in his hand.

"Spain and the Netherlands"

A page in the costume of the Age of Phillip IV evokes Velázquez and Murillo. The figure casts an admiring glance toward a lady holding a fan and attired in the "dress of people of elegance, as familiar from the portraits of Anthony van Dyck" (1599–1641).

"The Netherlands and Italian High Renaissance"

A cavalier in bearing and dress apparently borrowed from the paintings of Frans Hals (1582/83–1666) occupies the spandrel. His weapon is a rapier of Spanish provenience, and is possibly based on a group of similar type in the museum's Collection of Arms and Armour. Analogous to the motif in the preceding group, stands a page, here however, he appears in "Florentine dress". Behind the figure, a wedding casket may be seen, upon which rests a Majolica vase. The elegantly attired servant is shown taking a few flowers from the vase.

"Italian High Renaissance"

The lute player is inspired by "Bella" representations, of which Titian's *Violante* (c. 1510/15; Inv. No. 65) and Palma Vecchio's *Young Woman in Blue Gown* (c. 1512/14; Inv. No. 63) in the Picture Gallery are examples. In the spandrel on the right, a young man stands in the parade armour of the Duke of Parma, Alessandro Farnese, which was crafted in the workshop of Lucio Piccinino (c. 1578/79; KHM, Hofjagd- und Rüstkammer, Inv. No. A 1132).

Ernst Klimt, "The German Renaissance"

Ernst Klimt, "Spain and the Netherlands"

Ernst Klimt, "The Netherlands and Italian High Renaissance"

Ernst Klimt, "Italian High Renaissance"

"Northern Gothic of the Late Middle Ages"

The "Dance of Death" and legend of St. George: Matsch combines these "foremost ideas of Medieval art" into a coherent scene in the left spandrel and intercolumnar areas. Adam and Eve amplify the symbolism of the dragon as representative of sin. The style of the armour and the inscription above, which is painted such that only fragments are legible, both refer to Emperor Maximilian I. In the second spandrel, a "holy virgin of the type of St. Ursula" leans against its border holding her attributes sceptre and monstrance.

"Roman and Byzantine Art"

The youthful figure of an angel holds out a thurible. Matsch thus injects a dynamic element into the still-life which occupies the background. This is composed of two prominent works of Medieval goldsmiths' art, the reliquary bust of Charlemagne (after 1349) and the Shrine of the Virgin Mary (1220–38) in Aachen cathedral, the body of which projects into the spandrel. Against a splendid mosaic background, a female figure wearing a crown with pendilia and bearing a palm frond, and an ivory triptych symbolise the art of Byzantium.

"Ancient Rome"

The only partially visible inscription "Senatus Populusque Romanus" recalls the Roman republic, whilst the massive bronze statue, the *She-Wolf of the Capitol,* which looms in the spandrel's background, recalls the founding myth of the Eternal City. The female personification holds a statuette of the goddess of victory in her left hand, and a laurel wreath in her right. This intercolumnar area too is dominated by a still-life that represents imperial Rome with portrait busts and military insignia. The "paraphernalia of the Northern barbarian peoples […] who at the time began to make their appearance in the Empire's history" is also included in the picture.

Franz Matsch, "Northern Gothic of the Late Middle Ages"

Franz Matsch, "Roman and Byzantine Art"

Franz Matsch, "Ancient Rome"

"Carolingian and Burgundian Periods"

With Wagnerian pathos the blonde Germania contemplates the crown of the Holy Roman Empire (Second half of the tenth century; KHM, Kunstkammer, Weltliche Schatzkammer, Inv. No. XIII 1). She wears the coronation mantle (c. 1133/34, KHM, Kunstkammer, Inv. No. XIII 14) which is also preserved in the Schatzkammer. Both objects belong to the insignia of the Holy Roman Empire which Charlemagne founded in 800. This spandrel is located opposite the cupola hall. It thus forms a visual axis and iconographic counterpoint to the medallion of Franz Josef I found there, as well as to the Maria Theresia monument that dominates the plaza between the two museums.

The pair of lovers in the right spandrel – a youth bearing a pomegranate and a young woman attired in Burgundian court dress – refers to the "youthful Maximilian, who wed the beautiful Mary". Other references to Maximilian I are the emblems in the intercolumnar area: the double-headed eagle of the Holy Roman Empire surrounded by the collar of the Order of the Golden Fleece, and the coats of arms of Maximilian's parents below. Below to the right appears Amor, which is no doubt an allusion to the motto *bella gerant alii, tu felix Austria nube* ("May others make war, you happy Austria, marry").

"Florence of the Cinquecento and Quattrocento"

With the figure of Goliath in the intercolumnar field Klimt wished to allude to Michelangelo's *David* without however "citing the work itself". Below the decapitated head appears the Latin inscription which translated proclaims, "he who God would ruin, He first makes blind". To the right, the figure of Venus forms the female pendant.

"Baroque and Rococo"

Placed opposite one another in the intercolumnar areas flanking the spandrels, are the French king Louis XIV and Habsburg empress Maria Theresia based on their most characteristic portraits. Lorenzo Bernini's marble bust and Georg Raphael Donner's bronze served as models. In the spandrels a "gallant couple" appear to greet each other. The violin in the hand of the male figure may be a reference to the efflorescence of Viennese music during the age of Mozart.

Franz Matsch, "Carolingian and Burgundian Periods"

Gustav Klimt, "Florence of the Cinquecento and Quattrocento"

Franz Matsch, "Baroque and Rococo"

"Dutch and Flemish School"

A patrician lady holding a tulip represents the art of Rembrandt and Frans Hals. The "lecherous scene" to the right with bacchante and satyr, symbolises the painting of Rubens and Jacob Jordaens.

"Roman and Venetian Quattrocento"

In the intercolumnar area a basin for holy water, for which that of the cathedral of Siena served as model, and the "figure of a saint" wearing sumptuous pontifical robes represent Papal Rome of the early Renaissance. A woman with dark, wispy hair holds the Papal tiara in her hands. The doge in the right spandrel clearly owes its inspiration to Giovanni Bellini's famous portrait of Leonardi Loredan (c. 1501/04; London, National Gallery).

"Ancient Greece"

The young woman in the intercolumnar field "by chance in the manner of Tanagra figures", appears to enter the scene hesitantly. Behind her, a large bell krater represents the important ceramics holdings of the museum's Collection of Greek and Roman Antiquities. At the extreme right is the statuette *Venus Untying her Sandals* (see KHM, Antikensammlung, Inv. No. ANSA VI 340). As a compositional counterpart to "Ancient Egypt" (see above), Pallas Athena stands facing the viewer in a frontal pose; her shield providing a magnificent background that echoes the gold surfaces of the decoration surrounding the spandrels.

Ernst Klimt, "Dutch and Flemish School"

Gustav Klimt, "Roman and Venetian Quattrocento"

Gustav Klimt, "Ancient Greece"

Ceiling Painting

Hans Makart, *Triumph of Light Over Darkness,* sketch for ceiling painting. 1883/84. Vienna, Österreichische Galerie Belvedere, Inv. No. 3756 (© Österreichische Galerie Belvedere).

In 1887 the imperial court commissioned Mihály Munkácsy with the execution of a monumental ceiling painting. He was explicitly asked to take as his guide Makart's sketches and the completed fanlight paintings "in respect of the dimensions of the figures", "colouration" and "depth of gradation". In this way, a "harmonious whole" was to be created.[49] Munkácsy's numerous sketches however document the gradual abandonment of the approach adopted by Makart and Canon. A *Triumph of Light Over Darkness* dominated by tones of red, brown and gold, became an *Apotheosis of the Renaissance* set against a broad expanse of luminous blue into which an increasing number of architectural elements was integrated. This shift from mythology to what was essentially a realistic atelier scene is paralleled by that of the spandrels' design. Berger's ceiling painting too (see pp. 200 ff.) broke away in form and content from Neo-Baroque ideals. Munkácsy may never have seen the museum, which was close to completion at the time he received the commission. An appointment to pay a visit to the site on 1 November 1886 was most probably not kept, as the artist departed 6 November for New York in the company of his art dealer and returned to Paris only on 9 January of the following year. Regardless of whether Munkácsy later travelled to Vienna before completing the work in his Parisian atelier, he apparently possessed the information he required. The architectural backdrop shows beyond a general reliance on Raphael's *School of Athens,* distinct references to the museum's vestibule and staircase: a flight of marble stairs depicted in an exaggerated upward perspective rise toward a cupola, at whose vanishing point a loggia protrudes. At the cupola's highest point Munkácsy includes an oculus, a distinctive characteristic of the architecture of the museum's vestibule. A man depicted from the rear – easing thereby the viewer's access to the scene – enters the generously proportioned stage. On the first landing, to the left, Leonardo da Vinci and Raphael are engaged in discussion. On the right, behind the balustrade, Michelangelo appears in a classical pose representative of thought. On the second landing, Paolo Veronese works atop a scaffold on a large canvas. At the composition's centre, Titian instructs students in the painting of nude models.

In this classic atelier scene, which was the starting point for initial sketches and which faintly recalls Courbet's *The Artist's Studio* (1854/55; Paris, Musée d'Orsay), Munkácsy included himself above the head of the reclining model. In the central loggia above which the Medici coat of arms is to be seen, an elderly pope, possibly Clemens VII (Giulio de' Medici; reigned 1523–34) inspects designs presented by his artists.[50] Above this illustrious scene soar "Glory" and "Fame", personifying the honour and fame of art.

Mihály Munkácsy, *Apotheosis of the Renaissance*, painting on ceiling above staircase.

Cupola hall, general
view.

Cupola Hall

The cupola hall rises above an octagonal layout that extends over the museum's first and second floors. The plan is a clear allusion in form and significance to the Carolingian octagon of Aachen cathedral. Monumental pilasters with a massive base area form the powerful architectural frame. Atop these pilasters rests the cupola around which runs a gallery. The cupola as seen from within the building is not identical to that seen from outside, as a gap of approximately 20 metres separates the dome's interior and exterior apexes.

The area between the pilasters are occupied by round arches that extend over two stories and form an arcade, whose lower area is flanked by double columns. The upper spandrels of the round arches are populated by genii and figures of Fama executed in stucco. In the lower spandrels, sixteen "boys as allegories of the various artistic crafts" lend the sacral room a genre-like undertone. The iconographic centrepiece of the figural decoration, however, are the medallions and reliefs adorning the tambour of the cupola. Arranged in a collage-like fashion, they represent the political and cultural achievements of monarchs from Maximilian I to Franz Josef I, who were selected for the most part by Hasenauer and various curators. The portrait medallions are supported by personifications, below which appear horizontal stucco reliefs. The density of the allusions to Habsburg patronage of the arts is echoed in the extravagant richness of materials. Monochrome surfaces of different textures provide a foil to the figural decorative programme. The strictness of content is enlivened by many genre-like details. Architecturally the closed octagonal form sanctified by tradition is set off by numerous apertures.

One of the "boys as allegories of the various artistic crafts" by Rudolf Weyr in the spandrels of the cupola hall's vault.

Cupola hall, imitation marble surface.

Cupola hall, columns
of Porto Venere marble
behind which imitation
marble pillars can be seen.

Cupola hall, second floor
balcony.

Cupola hall, view of
double columns in the
arcades facing towards
cupola tambour.

Cupola reliefs
(Johannes Benk and Rudolf Weyr)

Genii (Carl Kundmann)

*"Boys as Allegories of the Various
Artistic Crafts"*
(Rudolf Weyr)

Cupola Reliefs

■ **Emperor Maximilian I**

1459–1518. Son of Emperor Ferdinand III and Eleonore of Portugal. First wife: Mary of Burgundy; son, Philip the Handsome, married to Joanna of Castile. Second wife: Bianca Maria Sforza. Grandfather of Karl V and Ferdinand I. King of the Romans 1486; Holy Roman Emperor 1508.

The allegorical figures of "Wood-Cutting" and "Metal Casting", which flank the effigy of the oldest of the Habsburgs represented in the cupola, recall supreme achievements of graphic arts and miniature painting during his reign *(Theuerdank, Freydal, Ehrenpforte),* as well as the monumental sculptural programme of his tomb. The relief below similarly refers to these aspects, depicting Maximilian as a young tournament rider, to the left a soldier of the period, canons, and an allusion to the armourer's craft that flourished in his time. To the right "Peace" and "Art" provide an appropriate counterweight to the skills of war and tournament. Albrecht Dürer and the architect of Vienna's St. Stephen's cathedral, Anton Pilgram, appear as important artistic figures of the age.

■ **Emperor Karl V**

1500–58. Son of Philip the Handsome and Joanna of Castile; elder brother of Emperor Ferdinand I and Maria of Hungary; grandson of Maximilian I. Married to Isabella of Portugal. Emperor 1519. Father of Philip II of Spain.

The portrayal of Karl V is less specific than that of Maximilian in its characterisation of the ruler's period. The supporters of the medallion bearing his likeness are straightforward and rather general: painting religious and secular. To the left, Albrecht Dürer's *Adoration of the Trinity* (1511, acquired 1585 by Rudolf II; KHM, Gemäldegalerie, Inv. No. 838) is to be seen, although neither the creation nor acquisition of the artwork is related to Karl V. The relief illustrates the relationship of patron and artist portraying the emperor engaged in discussion with Titian, who he appointed court painter in 1533. On the right, Weyr included the emperor's wife, Isabella of Portugal, his sister, Maria of Hungary; and his son, the Spanish king, Philip II, in a group portrait. In this manner the geographical extent of the Habsburg realms is visualised and more directly alluded to by globe, armillary sphere, and sailing ship.

Johannes Benk and Rudolf
Weyr, Emperor Maximilian I

Johannes Benk and Rudolf
Weyr, Emperor Karl V

Archduke Ferdinand of Tyrol

1529–95. Son of Ferdinand I and Anne of Bohemia and Hungary, brother of Maximilian II. Viceroy of Bohemia 1547. 1557 marriage to Philippine Welser († 1580). From 1564 ruler of Tyrol and Further Austria.

The allegorical figures represent the craft of weapon-making and the science of weaponry, the latter is depicted engaged in writing the *Armamentarium Heroicum,* a pictorial inventory of the Archduke's armoury in Ambras castle. These are a reference to Ferdinand's collecting enthusiasm and extensive interest in historical ceremonial armour and arms. His collecting activities established the core of the Collection of Arms and Armour that was exhibited in Kunsthistorisches Museum from its opening until 1935, when it was transferred to the Neue Burg.

The relief also refers to Emperor Maximilian I. As executor of his grandfather's testament, Ferdinand worked to complete his tomb in the Hofkirche in Innsbruck. Next to this is another allusion to the collection of arms. An image of Ambras castle, residence of Ferdinand and his wife Philippine Welser, looms in the background. To the right, Ferdinand and his wife are engaged in conversation with Alexander Colin, who created the sculptures and reliefs for Maximilian's tomb.

Emperor Rudolf II

1552–1612. Son of Emperor Maximilian II and Maria of Spain. Emperor 1576. Transfer of the imperial residence from Vienna to Prague 1583.

An antique bust and the "Amazon Sarcophagus" (KHM, Antikensammlung, Inv. No. ANSA I 169), only part of which is visible, bear witness to Rudolf's ambitions as collector. He endeavoured to acquire the sarcophagus, which was in the possession of the Fuggers; in the event he obtained what is probably a copy. The allegorical figure of goldsmiths' art on the right examines the crown of Rudolf II – later the Austrian Imperial Crown (1602; KHM, Kunstkammer, Weltliche Schatzkammer, Inv. No. WS XIa 1), which was crafted in the Prague atelier of Jan Vermeyen.

In the centre of the relief the emperor turns to his court astronomer, Tycho Brahe. Benvenuto Cellini's salt cellar, or *Saliera* (1540–43; KHM, Kunstkammer, Inv. No. KK 881) can be seen below to the right, next to which Adriaen de Vries (c. 1545/1560–1626), Rudolf's court sculptor, appears. In the group on the left, leaning upon the "Amazon Sarcophagus", is the numismatist, antique and art dealer, Jacopo Strada, who was active on behalf of Ferdinand I, Maximilian II and Rudolf II (see his portrait by Titians, c.1567/68; KHM, Gemäldegalerie, Inv. No. 81).

Johannes Benk and
Rudolf Weyr, Archduke
Ferdinand of Tyrol

Johannes Benk and Rudolf Weyr,
Emperor Rudolf II

Archduke Albrecht VII

1559–1621. Son of Emperor Maximilian II and Maria of Spain. Cardinal archbishop of Toledo 1577; viceroy of Portugal 1583–95; from 1599 together with his wife Isabella Clara Eugenia (married 1597), daughter of the Spanish king Philip II, governor general of the Spanish Netherlands.

Isabella Clara Eugenia, Albrecht's co-regent and wife succeeded in engaging Peter Paul Rubens, the foremost master of the Flemish Baroque, as court artist in 1608. Rubens is represented by one of his works *The Four Rivers of Paradise* (c. 1615; KHM, Gemäldegalerie, Inv. No. 526) to the left of the portrait medallion. The figure on the right symbolises numismatics.

This relief is an exception in that it does not include a portrait of the ruler and his wife. Albrecht's patronage is represented solely by paintings: Rubens' self-portrait with his first wife Isabella Brant (*The Honeysuckle Bower,* c. 1609; Munich, Alte Pinakothek), and Anthony van Dyck at work on the *Lamentation of Christ* (Munich, Alte Pinakothek).

Archduke Leopold Wilhelm

1614–62. Son of Emperor Ferdinand II and Maria Anna of Bavaria; he held a number of bishoprics, including those of Halberstadt and Olomouc. Commander-in-chief of the imperial armies in the Thirty Years' War 1639; governor general of the Spanish Netherlands 1646–56.

Leopold Wilhelm was the true founder of the Habsburg collection of paintings: some 1,400 of the Picture Gallery's works were originally belonged to him. This is referred to by the group to the left of the medallion in connection with genre painting, To the right, the art of tapestry appears; the highest quality examples were produced by the manufactories of Brussels in the sixteenth and seventeenth centuries.

The relief portrays Leopold Wilhelm and David Teniers and to their left, a company of merrymaking peasants, a reference to one of Teniers' favourite motifs, who was both painter and director of Archduke Leopold Wilhelm's gallery.

Johannes Benk and
Rudolf Weyr, Archduke
Albrecht VII

Johannes Benk and Rudolf
Weyr, Archduke Leopold
Wilhelm

Emperor Karl VI

1685–1740. Son of Emperor Leopold I and Eleonore of Pfalz-Neuburg; brother of Emperor Josef I († 1711). As king of Spain known as Carlos III. Married to Elisabeth Christine of Braunschweig-Wolfenbüttel. Emperor 1711.

The group to the left of the portrait medallion refers to Georg Raphael Donner's fountain depicting Providentia, or "Providence" (Vienna, Neuer Markt; original sculptures exhibited in the Lower Belvedere since 1921). The fountain was commissioned by the city of Vienna in 1737 and unveiled on the emperor's name day in 1739. To the right "Architecture" presents a plan of the Karlskirche (Johann Bernhard Fischer von Erlach, 1716–37). Construction of the church was initiated by Karl VI in 1713 following the last major plague epidemic.

The Karlskirche is cited in the relief again as an example of Vienna's architectural efflorescence under Karl VI. The continuous balustrade, both ends of which are guarded by sphinxes, alludes to another ambitious architectural project, the Belvedere palace built in 1716–23 for Prince Eugene of Savoy according to Johann Bernhard Fischer von Erlach's plans. The architect is shown in the group on the left next to the emperor and prince. The group on the right features Donner (1693–1741) with a model of the Providentia fountain, Daniel Gran (1694–1757), one of the leading Austrian painters of the Baroque, and Carl Gustav Heraeus (1671–1725?), imperial antiquarian, who designed the iconographic programme for the Karlskirche.

Emperor Franz Josef I

1830–1916. Son of Archduke Franz Karl and Sophie of Bavaria; grandson of Emperor Franz I (II). Emperor 1848. Marriage to Elisabeth of Bavaria 1854.

Alone among the portraits decorating the cupola, that of Franz Josef I is crowned by a laurel wreath. More clearly than in the seven other effigies, the winged genius on the left, who is recognizable as "Art" by the star above his forehead, and Vindobona (the Roman name for Vienna) face the imperial builder. The personification of Vienna sits atop the remnants of the city's fortifications, which were razed in 1857, whilst to the right a putto unrolls the plan for the capital's extension (1857 ff.).

The same theme is adopted in the relief: Franz Josef I indicates with a gesture of his hand the model of the imperial museums. Behind, the Maria Theresia monument is presented, whilst in the background the silhouette of Vienna city hall rises. To the right, a plan of the city extension signifies the emperor's major achievement in urban planning, architecture and, not least, in social and political fields. The chained figure of the Danube on the left edge symbolises the regulation of the river undertaken in 1870–75. On the right edge, a figure reclining upon reeds hands an exhausted labourer a bowl of water; this is a reference to construction of the first aqueduct (1870–73) to supply the capital with water from the Alps.

Johannes Benk and Rudolf
Weyr, Emperor Karl VI

Johannes Benk and Rudolf
Weyr, Emperor Franz Josef I

Galleries

"A wonderful impression is made by the views into the galleries with their endless succession of halls, and from the staircase to the entrance below."
Illustrierte Zeitung, Leipzig and Berlin, 18 December 1891, p. 689.

In designing the plan for the galleries Semper and Hasenauer were guided by a model, which had become part of the repertory of museum architecture for accommodating an extensive collection of paintings. This was established as a standard at the latest with the opening of the Alte Pinakothek in Munich (1836). The scheme combined large exhibition halls with a series of smaller rooms or "cabinets". In the museum in Vienna the symmetrical plan has rooms running around two interior courtyards separated by the representative central axis. On the ground floor, the large halls face the outside, and the cabinets accordingly the inner courtyard. In the floor above, in the Picture Gallery, this arrangement is reversed. Here skylights provide light for the large windowless halls, whilst the adjacent cabinets are equipped with windows.

The walls separating the halls and cabinets of the Picture Gallery thus lie over the centre of the halls below on the ground floor. Semper solved this structural problem by use of columns or pillars, which very largely determine the impression that the rooms make. The original installation of the collections is reflected in the rooms' decoration, which is of a superlative artistic and scholarly standard.

The building was designed in 1871 to be lit by natural light. Originally there may have been gas mains in some areas of the basement. In the 1880s it was probably technically possible to make use of electric light. As early as the 1850s South Kensington Museum (later the Victoria and Albert Museum) had introduced gas lighting in the picture galleries. By 1890 artificial light had apparently been developed that satisfactorily compensated for its drawbacks compared to natural light (reflections, generation of heat, distracting shadows). Trailblazer in the use of this technology – already specialized for the presentation of paintings and promoted as such at international fairs – was again England. The British Museum in London introduced electric lighting in some of its galleries in 1890.

Egyptian and Near Eastern Collection, Hall I, c. 1910. Vienna, Österreichische Nationalbibliothek, Picture Archive, Inv. No. PCH 2.153 (© Österreichische Nationalbibliothek).

1891

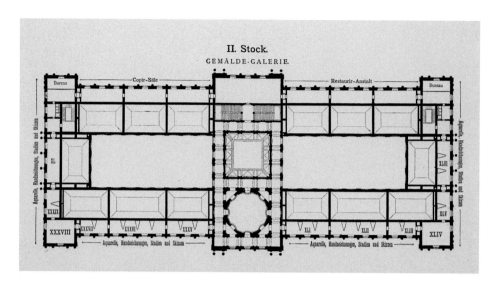

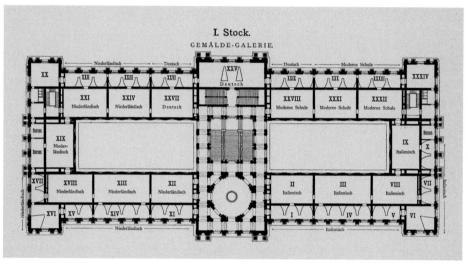

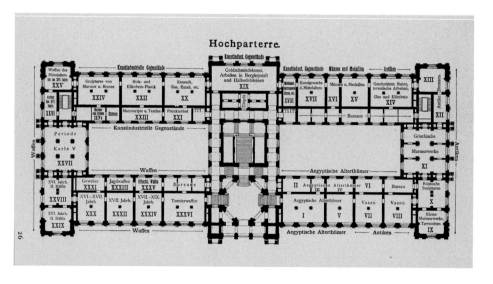

From: *Übersicht der kunsthistorischen Sammlungen des
allerhöchsten Kaiserhauses,*
Vienna, 1891.

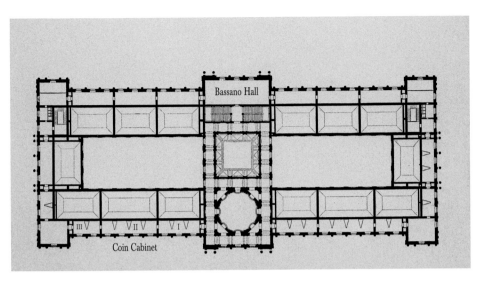

Bassano Hall

Coin Cabinet

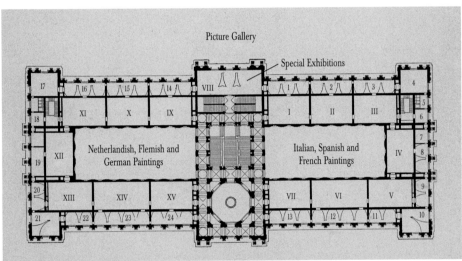

Picture Gallery

Special Exhibitions

Netherlandish, Flemish and
German Paintings

Italian, Spanish and
French Paintings

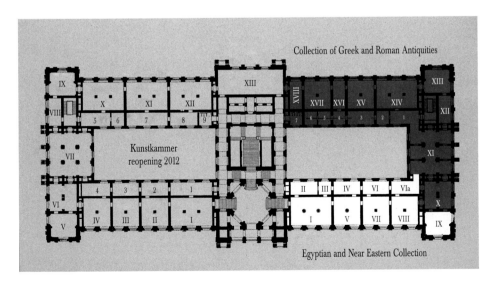

Collection of Greek and Roman Antiquities

Kunstkammer
reopening 2012

Egyptian and Near Eastern Collection

"Egyptian Antiquities"
Egyptian and Near Eastern Collection

The romantic Egyptomania that arose in the wake of Napoleon's Egyptian campaign, and was further stimulated by the deciphering of hieroglyphics in 1822, gave birth to a field of study represented in the German-speaking countries by Richard Lepsius (1810–84). In 1842–45 the Egyptologist led an expedition financed by the Prussian king. The expedition's rich booty of some 1,500 objects was exhibited in the Neues Museum in Berlin, which was constructed in 1843–45 and designed to present them in an appropriate fashion. The Neues Museum was a prominent precursor which provided a guide to the display of Egyptian art. The core of the Berlin institution was the "Egyptian Court", a one-third scale reconstruction of the hypostyle hall of the Ramesseum in Karnak. Wall paintings of pedagogic character completed the exotic staging. Lepsius and Stüler thus established a new model for the museum: the old "historical-philosophical concept" was now replaced by the "historical didactic".[51] The enjoyment of art, which had until then been regarded as the central criteria for a museum, now gave way to "education through history". A practical disadvantage to a scheme of interior decoration closely related to the objects exhibited became manifest only in the decades that followed. The growth of special collections and the transfer of entire groups of holdings to new quarters did violence to the original relationship between interior decoration and exhibits. Among other factors, this problem which was the subject of public discussion, may have led Semper and Hasenauer to favour a decorative programme of a more general character without a direct relationship to the objects exhibited.

The wall decorations for Halls I, II and V already existed at the time work on the interior commenced. Ernst Weidenbach (1818–82), the son of a German landscape painter, had accompanied Lepsius on the expedition financed by the Prussian king. In August 1843, they reached Beni Hassan. One of the tombs of the necropolis, which is among the most important archaeological sites in Middle Egypt, was exhaustively documented. Lepsius commissioned Weidenbach to prepare tracings of the paintings found in the tomb of the nomarch Khnumhotep II.[52] The drawings served both as material for a scientific publication and for the decoration of the Egyptian pavilion at the Vienna World Exhibition of 1873.[53] The large scale reproductions on paper that were produced were placed at the disposal of Kunsthistorisches Museum after the World Exhibition closed. As chief architect of the event in Vienna's Prater, Hasenauser enjoyed direct access to the reproductions.

In selecting and designing the other motifs, architects and craftsman could in addition to Lepsius' publication, refer to a great number of pattern books. With the

Overleaf, double page:
Egyptian and Near Eastern
Collection, Hall I

Egyptian and Near Eastern
Collection, Hall I

inauguration of the Suez Canal in 1869, a new wave of Egyptomania took hold adding a popular enthusiasm for all things Egyptian now complemented scholarly study. In the years that followed, innumerable articles of everyday use in the ancient Egyptian style were industrially produced.[54]

Haal I

Egyptian and Near Eastern Collection, Hall I, detail of the wall decorations by Ernst Weidenbach, after the northern wall of the tomb of Khnumhotep II.

Among the rooms (Halls I–VI) originally foreseen for the Egyptian Collection, Hall I was the most extensively decorated with wall paintings from the World Exhibition. A painting intended for a burial chamber was necessarily divorced from its context. Individual registers had to make way for the large windows, and others for the high showcases. As a consequence, some motifs for which no space was available were

used in Halls II and V. On the wall with the doorway which affords access to
Hall V, Weidenbach's copy shows an extract from the north wall of the tomb of
Khnumhotep II.

To the left, extending over three registers, the deceased can be seen hunting in the
desert for antelope, hyenas, foxes, leopards, lions, hedgehogs, and jerboa. Behind
Khnumhotep are six servants hunting gazelles, as well as three others with weapons
and hunting dogs. In the two uppermost registers, four of Khnumhotep's sons are
engaged in hunting with bows and arrows. To the right, the deceased is portrayed as
spectator, to whom the activities he is watching relate. A caravan of Asiatics with
lute players and donkeys loaded down with goods and children approach. The
inscription records that they are bearing eye makeup for the nomarch, "in the sixth

year of the majesty of Horus, the unifier of both lands, king of Upper and Lower Egypt, Sesostris II: the number of Aamu which were brought by the son of Count Khnumhotep for eye makeup, amounts to thirty-seven Aamu from the neighbouring country of Shu". In 1869, the imperial house had received a gift of three papyrus columns produced during the Twelfth Dynasty of the Middle Kingdom (2137–1761 B.C.) and later emblazoned with the inscriptions of Thutmose IV, Merenptah I, and Seti II. The archaeological finds had first been offered to Maximilian of Mexico for a new museum planned for Miramar palace. Only after Maximilian's death did the columns' Venetian owner offer them to Franz Josef.[55] They were transported to Vienna by way of Trieste and first exhibited in the Lower Belvedere. In 1876 they were integrated into the new museum as a supporting element.

The barrel vaults of Halls I and V are adorned with flying vultures as the personification of the lands and crown of Upper Egypt. This decorative motif was originally reserved to royal tombs. Here it is based on the representation found in the tomb of the vizier Bakenrenef in Saqqara (Twenty-Sixth Dynasty, c. 650 B.C.). Floral forms as a symbol of life and growth were held in high esteem and employed extensively in tomb decorations. Such ornamentation can be seen on the ceilings of Halls II (papyrus umbels) and Hall III (lilies and papyrus blossoms in combination with rosettes). The winged scarab – here depicted together with papyrus umbels (Hall IV) – was the sacred animal of the sun god and also the symbol of resurrection and life. The door frames, lectern and wall showcases (the work of Vinzenz Hefele and the Falkenstein workshop) lend the exhibition halls with a uniform appearance.

Egyptian and Near Eastern Collection, Hall V, decoration of scarabs for ceiling, executed by the Falkenstein workshop, 1889.

Opposite:
Egyptian and Near Eastern Collection, Hall I, ceiling decoration after those found in the tomb of Bakenrenef, Saqqara No. 24, 664–610 B.C., Chamber C.

Collection of Greek and Roman Antiquities, Hall X, c. 1910. Vienna, Österreichische Nationalbibliothek, Picture Archive, Inv. No. PCH 2155/STE (© Österreichische Nationalbibliothek).

"The Ancient World"

Collection of Greek and Roman Antiquities

Hall VII in which part of the Egyptian and Near Eastern Collection is now displayed, originally housed the collection of antique vases. These were for the most part kept in the Augustine Passageway, more precisely, in the Imperial Coin and Antiquities Cabinet, in the Hofburg imperial palace until 1890.

The decoration and paintings allude in restrained fashion to the collection. Differently than in the preceding rooms of the Egyptian and Near Eastern Collections, only the ceiling area is decorated thus allowing flexibility in changing the collections exhibited in the hall irrespective of the objects to be displayed. The vault, like those in most of the other exhibition halls, is decorated according to a uniform scheme

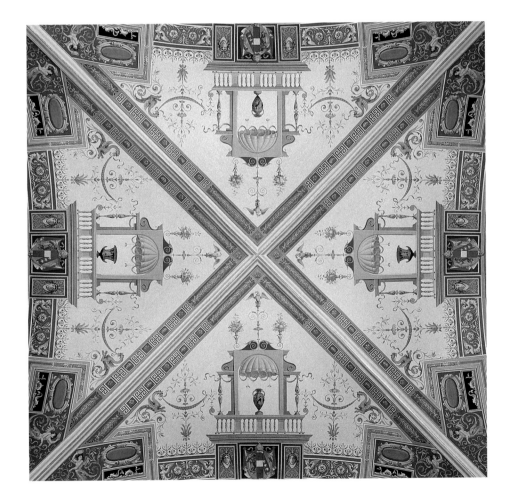

Formerly the Collection of Greek and Roman Antiquities, today Egyptian and Near Eastern Collection, Hall VII, vault decoration, detail.

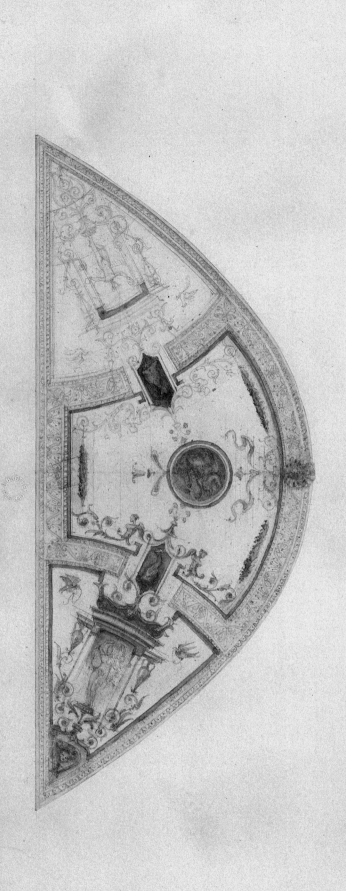

G Semper f 1875.

enhanced by more specific elements and paintings are added. The grotesques on the vault's ribs and surfaces clearly echo the best-known revival of ancient Roman ornament, Raphael's decoration of the Vatican loggias (1508 ff.). In part too, the grotesques are direct copies of the decoration of the Sala Ducale in the Vatican. Semper in fact travelled to Genoa to study arabesque decoration there.

Oriented to the apex of the vaults is a representation of a delicate baldachin on whose dais appear the arms of Habsburg-Lorraine. Beneath the baldachin is a chalice krater and amphora of late Panathenaic type. The chalice krater with its large opening and upward pointed handles was used to mix wine and water. The model for the vessel depicted here was the krater of Agrigento picturing Theseus before Poseidon and Amphitrite (Bibliothèque Nationale, Paris) or a vessel of the type of late Panathenaic prize amphorae.

Collection of Greek and Roman
Antiquities, Hall XIII, new installation of Roman busts, 2006.

Hall IX and Hall XIII

Originally reserved for the "monuments of Classical art", but today housing both part of the Egyptian and Near Eastern Collection and Collection of Greek and Roman Antiquities, Hall IX and at the opposite end of the building's narrow side, Hall XIII, together comprise a formal unit. The decorative and colour schemes of the ceilings of the two rooms are identical.

The iconographic programme for the ceilings of both halls was designed by Robert von Schneider (1854–1909), who from 1876 worked in the Imperial Coin and Antiquities Cabinet and was appointed director of the Antiquities Collection in 1900. His concept was based on the periodisation of Greek art introduced by Joachim Winckelmann (1717–68), which from today's perspective must be deemed too decidedly judgmental. In the "Older Style" (sixth century) Egyptian influence is still perceptible. The "High Style" (Phidias, fifth century) and "Beautiful Style" (Praxiteles and Lysippos, fourth century) mark the highpoint of an organic development, which was followed, in Winckelmann's interpretation, by a decline of style and civilisation.[56] Schneider selected charites as the epitome of the "High Style" (Hall IX) and "Beautiful Style" (Hall XIII; ceiling: "Beautiful Style", Pothos and Himeros, Eos, Hesperus; in the fanlight, a view of the heroon of Gölbaşi-Trysa). The artist of the canvases executed for mounting in the ceiling fields was with but a single exception Karl Karger (1848–1913). In 1886, the painter of genre and historical scenes completed one of his principal works with ceiling paintings for the vestibules of the boxes in the Court Theatre. The fanlight paintings in Halls IX and XIII are by Robert Russ (1847–1922), hailed by contemporary art critics as the "master of lighting effects" and Ludwig Hans Fischer (Hall XIII).

Karl Karger, ceiling paintings, Collection of Greek and Roman Antiquities, Hall IX, "High Style" and Eros and Penia.

Formerly the Collection of Greek and Roman Antiquities, Hall IX, today Egyptian and Near Eastern Collection.

Karger summarised early Classicism's strict ideas of form in a very general manner, choosing for the "High Style" a backdrop with the ruins of a Doric temple. A charis clothed in a white peplos rests upon the stylobate, the uppermost level of the stepped platform of a Greek temple, which here serves to divide the polygon into two halves. An amphora at her feet, Charis gazes down with sovereign demeanour at the viewer below.

The rectangular picture shows Eros and Penia (Roman: Paupertas) the personification of poverty, mother of effort and perseverance. According to Plato, Penia stole the semen of Poros, the god of abundance, in order to give birth to Eros (Roman: Amor, the god of sexual love). In older Greek mythology Penia was considered the instructor of industriousness and the arts. In the tondi to the right and left of the grisaille appears Helios, the Greek sun god, and his sister Selena (Roman: Luna), the moon goddess, with the orb of the moon in the background. The view of Samothrace makes a direct reference to the imperial collections. The German archaeologist Alexander Conze had drawn attention to the importance of the northern Aegean island in the 1850s. In 1863, French archaeologists unearthed the famed "Winged Victory of Samothrace" (Paris, Musée du Louvre). In 1873, Conze, who already taught at the University of Vienna, was able to persuade the Austrian government to finance research and began excavations.

Robert Russ, View of Samothrace, Collection of Greek and Roman Antiquities, Hall IX.

Karl Karger, ceiling painting, Collection of Greek and Roman Antiquities, Hall IX, Helios and Selena.

Hall X

Since reinstallation of the Collection of Greek and Roman Antiquities in 2006, Hall X has been devoted to the sculpture of ancient Greece. In 1891, the room was first used to exhibit "sculpture in stone". This rather broad purpose had for good reason no influence on the decorative programme of the ceiling, and inspiration was

Collection of Greek and Roman Antiquities, Hall X, new installation of Greek sculpture, 2006.

sought in a general symbolism. The director of the Collection, Robert Schneider, used the opportunity to showcase the foundations of his own academic discipline, "all the [...] representations are conceived as female figures in antique costumes, similar to the muses who in antique painting are invariably portrayed clothed. [...] it is to be most earnestly wished that as symbols or accoutrements used as accessories there be depictions of famous objects from the Imperial collections.[57] The study of the "ideal" and "true" fields is also represented: "Archaeology" is accompanied by one of its most important primary sources, "Mythology", as well as by an ancillary discipline, "Iconography". "History" is portrayed in the company of "Numismatics" and "Epigraphy". Franz Xaver Simm (1853–1918) received the commission for the works. Simm, who in 1869–76 had studied under Anselm Feuerbach, a major German painter of the second half of the nineteenth century, was active principally as an illustrator.

Collection of Greek and Roman Antiquities, Hall X, ceiling with paintings by Franz Xaver Simm.

Franz Xaver Simm

1. *"Archaeology"*: The bronze leg of a table with busts of Attis (Roman, early empire, first century A.D., Collection of Greek and Roman Antiquities, Inv. No. ANSA VI 1685); column krater: Triptolemus between Demeter and Persephone (Greek, Attic, red figure, mid-fifth century B.C.; KHM, Antiken-sammlung, Inv. No. ANSA VI 641); statue of Isis (Roman, Middle Imperial Period, first half of second century A.D.; Inv. No. ANSA I 158); *Venus Untying her Sandals* (Roman, Early Imperial Period, after a Hellenistic original, c. 200 B.C., Inv. No. ANSA VI 340).

2. *"Mythology"*:
Aphrodite of Aphrodisias (Roman, Middle Imperial Period, second century A.D.; KHM, Antiken-sammlung, Inv. No. ANSA I 139).

3. *"Iconography"*:
The allegory compares the bust of an as yet unidentified figure with the portrayal on a coin.

Overleaf: Collection of Greek and Roman Antiquities, Hall XI.

4. *"History"*:
The sun-dial on the left alludes to the passing of time. The chronicler intently observes the battle in progress in the background

5. *"Epigraphy"*:
The allegorical depiction of the study of inscriptions inspects the "Tombstone from Nona" (second century A.D.; KHM, Antiken-sammlung, Inv. No. III 85).

6. *"Numismatics"*:
The bust on the right is of Hilarius Eckhel (1737–98), the founder of the numismatics as a science. In 1774 Eckhel became director of the collection of ancient coins of the Imperial Coin and Antiquities Cabinet. The figure of "Numis-matics" gazes at the "Allegory of Moneta".

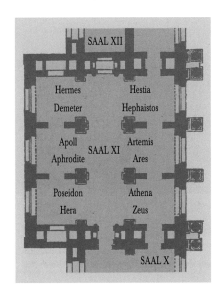

Hall XI

The articulation of the ceiling in the preceding and following rooms with lunettes, grotesques and arabesques, also dominates the median axis of the "Roman Hall". To the right and left of this axis, a different decorative scheme unfolds. Three coffered barrel vaults lying at right angles to the median axis lend the halls a monumental quality. Walls with apertures and barrel vaults recall the most momentous innovations of Roman architecture, the use of arches and vaults. Here in particular, the stylistic affinity with the interior architecture of Semper's Dresden gallery (1847–55) is evident. The objects to be exhibited in the rooms determined their decoration: the brilliantly treated stucco surfaces of the sensitively coloured (dividing) walls remain undecorated up to their beams. Whilst in the Egyptian Collections original papyrus columns were used, here the architects integrated the mosaic of Theseus and the Minotaur (Inv. No. ANSA II 20), which was discovered in a Roman "Villa on the Loigerfelder" near Salzburg, into the centre of the marble floor. The paintings are the work of August Eisenmenger (1830–1907), a student at the Vienna Academy of the Visual Arts and from 1845, from 1856 a student of Karl Rahl. Eisenmenger was responsible for frescoes and ceiling paintings in Musikverein, Parliament, Burgtheater, and City Hall. The surrounding frieze shows the twelve Olympians, the principal gods of Greek and Roman mythology, each with characteristic scenes and figures.

Zeus (Jupiter); Ganymede; Zeus in the Battle of the Titans with Nike and Athena; Chronos; Rape of Europa; Hebe.
Hera (Iuno); Athena Promachos; Zeus, Hera, Heracles, Hebe, Rhea; Zeus and Hera, Marital Dispute; Persephone.
Athena (Minerva); Athena with her holy serpent; Athena and Poseidon; Nike; Perseus and the Medusa; Athena and Erichthonius.
Poseidon (Neptune); Nymph/Nereid; Poseidon and Amphitrite; Oceanus; Tritones and Nereids; Nymph/Nereid.
Ares (Mars); Eris; Ares and Aphrodite; Ares/Heros; Mars and the Sleeping Rhea Silvia; Heracles/Hercules.
Aphrodite (Venus); Psyche; Birth of Aphrodite; Aphrodite Kallipygos; Hippomenes and Atalante; Eros.
Apollo (Apollo); Hyacinth; Flaying of Marsyas; Asclepius; Orpheus among the Shepherds; Daphne.
Artemis (Diana); Endymion; Sacrifice of Iphigenia; Artemis Soteria; Artemis and Actaeon; Niobids.

Hall XI, schematic plan of frieze locations.

Opposite: Collection of Greek and Roman Antiquities, Hall XI, view through to Cabinet 1 with part of the frieze depicting the gods by August Eisenmenger.

Collection of Greek and Roman Antiquities, Hall XI, decoration of hall's median axis, detail.

Hephaestus (Vulcanus); Hephaestus; Thetis and Hephaestus; Hephaestus; Birth of Athena; Prometheus.

Demeter (Ceres); Persephone Kore; Dispatch of Triptolemus; Satyr; Dionysus and his Retinue; Pluto/Hades and Cerberus.

Hestia (Vesta); Pandora; Horae; Nemesis; Pegasus and the Muses; Moira.

Hermes (Merkur); Pan; Hermes Psychopompos; Hermes; The Judgement of Paris; Hermaphroditus.

Previous double page:
Collection of Greek and Roman Antiquities, Hall XI, in the foreground on the left, the Amazon Sarcophagus (Greek, second half of fourth century B.C., AS Inv. No. I 169).

Collection of Greek and Roman Antiquities, view from Cabinet 6 to the Youth from Magdalensberg (16th century cast after Roman original, bronze, Antikensammlung Inv. No. VI) in Cabinet 7, new installation, 2006 (design: Hans Hoffer).

Collection of Greek and Roman Antiquities, Hall XVII, walk-in display area for the treasure of Nagyszentmiklós (eighth to ninth centuries A.D., Antikensammlung Inv. No. VII B 33) and other objects, new installation, 2006 (design: Hans Hoffer).

"Collection of Sculpture and Decorative Arts"
Kunstkammer

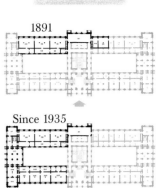

The Collection of Arms and Armour was transferred from Kunsthistorisches Museum to the Neue Burg on Heldenplatz in the 1930s. The Collection of Sculpture and Decorative Arts (renamed "Kunstkammer" in 1991) has since occupied more than half the ground floor, or approximately 2,700 square metres. Financial resources were last available for a reinstallation in 1979. A new concept for the collection's exhibition as well as a technical upgrade of the infrastructure, have thus become ever more pressing concerns in recent years. The museum's unique holdings of sculptures, goldsmiths' work, ceremonial and stone vessels, bronze figurines, turned ivories, and tapestries have thus not been accessible to the public since 2002. The Kunstkammer is scheduled to reopen in 2012.

Gregor van der Schardt, Allegory of the Four Seasons, Nuremberg, c. 1569/78, Kunstkammer storeroom.

Kunstkammer, former Hall XXIV (future Hall X), c. 1910, Österreichische Nationalbibliothek, Vienna, Picture Archive, Inv. No. PCH 2164 (© Österreichische Nationalbibliothek).

Kunstkammer, Hall XVII (today Hall XVII, Antikensammlung), c. 1910, Österreichische Nationalbibliothek, Vienna, Picture Archive, Inv. No. PCH 2175/STE (© Österreichische Nationalbibliothek).

Previous double page:
"Kunstindustrielle Gegenstände",
former Hall XXIV, "Sculpturen
von Marmor und Bronce" (future
Hall X, Kunstkammer), condition
in 2007.

Kunstkammer, former Hall XIX,
"Goldschmiedekunst, Arbeiten in
Bergkrystall und Halbedelsteinen"
(future Hall XIII), c. 1910. Österrei-
chische Nationalbibliothek (ANL),
Vienna, Picture Archive, Inv. No.
PCH 2159 Btc (© Österreichische
Nationalbibliothek).

Hall XIII ("Golden Hall")

The ceiling painting by Julius Berger in the "Golden Hall", the largest hall on the
ground floor, at once underscores the representative character of the sequence of
rooms located on its axis (vestibule-staircase-cupola hall). The painting continues
the decorative scheme used in the other galleries, which centres around the objects
displayed.

The wide-angle perspective, architectonically dramatic foreground of stairs, and
"cultivated colouristic treatment" succeed in creating, despite the painting's pletho-
ra of iconographic requirements, figures and objects, a harmonious whole. The
lions that guard the staircase and the figures of Victoria, also to be seen on the
museum's façade are included as recognisable citations in the idealising architecture of the painting. The museum's builder Emperor Franz Josef, to whom a direct
reference is made at the upper end of the central baldachin, indirectly plays a
principal role: "his" house offers stage and shelter to the "entire" history of art.
Julius Berger studied under Hans Makart. A scholarship permitted him to finance
a sojourn in Italy from 1874 to 1877. He taught at the School of Industrial Arts in
1881–87, where Gustav Klimt was one of his students. In the history of nineteenth-
century Viennese painting Berger is something of an intermediary. Turning away
from the Neo-Baroque works of Makart's followers and adopting Classicist
tendencies, he prepared the ground for a young generation of painters around
1900. Berger's *œuvre* consists mostly of depictions of historical events and wall or
ceilings murals. His chief work was the decoration (1880) of the Festsaal of the
Palace of Justice in Vienna (constructed 1875–81), which however was to remain
unexecuted. The concept for the ceiling painting, including stylistic recommenda-
tions, was Albert Ilg's. Berger was to portray a "more serene and symmetrical
gathering", "paradigmatic reference points" were to be derived from Raphael's
Disputation of the Holy Sacrament and depictions of the *Sacra Conversazione* by the "old
Venetians".[58]

In fact however, the models for the painting are to be found in rather less venera-
ble French and Belgian works of the nineteenth century: Jean Auguste Domi-
nique Ingres (1780–1867) *Apotheosis of Homer* (1827; Paris, Musée du Louvre),
Hippolyte Delaroche (1797–1856) hemicycle in the École des Beaux-Arts (1841–42;
Paris, École Nationale Supérieure des Beaux-Arts) and quite directly paintings by
Nicaise de Keyser (1813–87) for the Antwerp Academy (allegorical representation
of the city of Antwerp surrounded by artists of the Gothic and Renaissance,
1862–72; Antwerp, Musée Royal des Beaux-Arts).

1 Gasparo Miseroni[59]
Around 1518–73. Engraver of gems from Milan; founder of a workshop of his name, which was later also active in Prague during the reign of Emperor Rudolf II.

2 Emperor Rudolf II
1552–1612; Kaiser 1576. After a painting by Hans von Aachen (1606/08; KHM, Gemäldegalerie, Inv. No. 6438).

3 Jacopo Strada
1515–1588. After a painting by Titian (c. 1567/68, KHM, Gemäldegalerie, Inv. No. 81).

4 Crown of Emperor Rudolf II, later Austrian Imperial Crown
At the time the painting was executed the crown was attributed to Altenstetter, today it is deemed to be the work of Jan Vermeyen (KHM, Kunstkammer, Inv. No. WS XIa 1).

5 David Altenstetter
Alternately known under the names Altenstadt, Altenstedter, Attemstett, Attemstetter. Enamel artist and goldsmith; c. 1547–1617; court goldsmith to Emperor Rudolf II.

6 Leone Leoni
1509–90. Sculptor, medallist and goldsmith; worked for Emperor Karl V.

7 Valerio Belli[60]
1468–1546. Goldsmith and engraver of gems from Vicenza.

8 Benvenuto Cellini
1500–72. Studied the goldsmith's craft in Florence, Siena, Bologna and Rome; 1529 master die-cutter at the Papal mint; active for a brief period at the court of the French king François I (1494–1547).

9 Salt Cellar, "Saliera"
The only authenticated work in gold by Cellini; created 1540-43 for the French king François I (KHM, Kunstkammer, Inv. No. KK 881).

10 Joanello (Gianello) Torriani[61]
1500–85. Mathematician and watchmaker.

11 Jean Boulogne, called Giambologna
1529–1608. Sculptor; next to him on the parapet, "Astronomy" (c. 1573; Inv. No. KK 5893); *Hercules Slays the Centaur* (Antonio Susini after Giambologna, c. 1600; KHM, Kunstkammer, Inv. No. KK 5834).

12 Unidentified

13 Titian
Around 1488/90–1576. After one of the artist's self-portraits (1546/47 [?], Berlin, Staatliche Museen, Gemäldegalerie).

14 Emperor Karl V.
1500–58, emperor 1519–56. In clothing and type the depiction draws on the portrait in Alte Pinakothek, Munich, traditionally ascribed to Titian, but today is attributed to an occasional member of his workshop, Lambert Sustris.

15 Isabella of Portugal
1503–39. Wife of Emperor Karl V. After a portrait by Titian (1548, Madrid, Museo del Prado).

16 Maria of Hungary
1505–1558. Sister of Emperor Karl V, queen of Bohemia and Hungary, governor of the Netherlands.

17 Francesco Terzi
Around 1523–91. Painter, draughtsman for engravings and woodcuts, etcher; Court artist to Ferdinand of Tyrol. Illustrator of *Imagines Gentis Austriacae,* an ambitious and partially fictitious engraved genealogy of the Habsburg dynasty, executed 1558–71.

18 Giovanni Battista Serabaglio named Panzeri[62]
Active c. 1560/70 in Milan. Embosser; worked for Archduke Karl II of Inner Austria (see KHM, Hofjagd- und Rüstkammer, Inv. Nos. HJRK A 936; HJRK A 747; Kunstkammer, Inv. No. KK 879).

19 Lucio Piccinino
Active c. 1575 until after 1595 in Milan. Goldsmith, embosser (see, for example, KHM, Hofjagd- und Rüstkammer, Inv. No. HJRK A 1132)

JUL.BERGER

(20) Archduke Ferdinand II of Tyrol
1529–95, son of Emperor Ferdinand I and Anna of Bohemia and Hungary, brother of Emperor Maximilian II. 1547–63 governor of Bohemia, from 1565 regent in Tyrol. Married Philippine Welser († 1580) secretly in 1557. Second marriage in 1582 to Anna Caterina Gonzaga. He is shown holding Emperor Karl V's burgonet *all'antica* in the form of a lion's head (Filippo Negroli, um 1541, KHM, Hofjagd- und Rüstkammer, Inv. No. HJRK A 693), which he acquired for the armoury at Schloss Ambras.

(21) Still-life
Composed of the following objects:
Rock crystal bowl (Milan c. 1580, KHM, Kunstkammer, Inv. No. KK 2235); round shield from the "Milanese Armour" made for Archduke Ferdinand II of Tyrol (Giovanni Battista Serabaglio named Panzeri, 1559, KHM, Collection of Arms and Armour, Inv. No. HJRK A 785); Nautilus Goblet (1591; KHM, Kunstkammer, Inv. No. KK 1176); vessel of lapis lazuli (1575/76–1581, KHM, Kunstkammer, Inv. No. KK 1655); ceremonial rapier of Emperor Maximilian II (c. 1550, KHM, Collection of Arms and Armour, Inv. No. HJRK A 588); burgonet from the "Roman Armour" made for Archduke Ferdinand of Tyrol (Filippo Negroli (?), c. 1545/50, KHM, Hofjagd- und Rüstkammer, Inv. No. HJRK A 783).

(22) Gilg Sesselschreiber
Around 1460/65 – after 1520. Sketches for the forty planned statues for the tomb of Emperor Maximilian I.

(23) Hans Springinklee[63]
1490/95 – c. 1540. Painter and illustrator; pupil and collaborator of Albrecht Dürer. Worked on the *Ehrenpforte* and *Weisskunig* for Emperor Maximilian I.

(24) Johannes Stabius[64]
Around 1460–1522. Humanist, scientist and historian. 1498–1503 professor of mathematics in Ingolstadt, in 1503 Konrad Celtis called Stabius to the university in Vienna, at the same time he entered the service of Maximilian I as advisor in scientific and literary matters. He was the author of significant parts of the *Ehrenpforte* and *Triumphzug*.

(25) Emperor Maximilian I
1459–1518. Son of Emperor Ferdinand III and Eleonore of Portugal; 1486 King of the Romans, 1508 emperor; after a portrait by Albrecht Dürer (1519; KHM, Gemäldegalerie, Inv. No. GG 825).

(26) Albrecht Dürer
1471–1528. After a self-portrait (1500, Munich, Alte Pinakothek).

(27) Alexander Colin[65]
Around 1527–1612. Created the statue of the kneeling Emperor Maximilian I (1582), the four cardinal virtues (1569), and most of the alabaster reliefs for the emperor's tomb in Innsbruck.

(28) Hans Burgkmair the Elder[66]
1473–1531. Together with Hans Holbein the Younger the most important Augsburg artist of his time; series of woodcuts for the *Weisskunig*.

(29) Archduke Leopold Wilhelm
1614–1662. Son of Emperor Ferdinand II and Maria Anna of Bavaria. With Emperor Rudolf II, he played the major role in acquiring the Habsburg collection of paintings: some 1,400 of the works currently part of the Picture Gallery come from his collection. After a portrait by Peter Thys (probably in 1650s, KHM, Gemäldegalerie, Inv. No. GG 370).

(30) Adriaen Brouwer[67]
1605/06–38. Flemish painter of genre scenes, which frequently have a caricaturist quality and are set in a rural milieu or taverns. His work was appreciated by both Rubens and Rembrandt and influenced among other artists, David Teniers the Younger, court painter to Archduke Leopold Wilhelm.

(31) David Teniers the Younger
1610 (?)–90. From 1650 court painter to Archduke Leopold Wilhelm; compiled the *Theatrum Pictorium* (1660) and painted gallery scenes for his patron (see KHM, Gemäldegalerie, Inv. No. 739). Founder of the Antwerp Academy of Fine Arts (1664).

(32) Jacob Prandtauer[68]
1660–1726. Architect; principal work, Melk abbey, 1702 f. (Baroque reconstruction completed 1736).

33 Ybbs
One of four personifications of Austrian rivers executed for the Providentia fountain (Neuer Markt; originals in the Lower Belvedere), which was commissioned in 1737 by the city of Vienna and unveiled in 1739 on the name day of Emperor Karl VI.

34 Emperor Karl VI.
1685–1740. Son of Emperor Leopold I and Eleonore of Pfalz-Neuburg. Known as Carlos III as Spanish king; emperor 1711. After the portrait by Johann Friedrich Auerbach (KHM, Gemälde-galerie, Inv. No. 1801). A page presents the illustrated inventory of the imperial collections commissioned by the emperor and compiled by Ferdinand Storffer (three volumes published, 1720, 1730, 1733).

35 Prince Eugene of Savoy-Carignan
1663–1736. General and patron of the arts. Commander-in-chief of the imperial armies during the wars against the Ottomans; took part in the War of the Spanish Succession; major building commissions included the Belvedere and winter palace in the Himmelpfortgasse in Vienna.

36 Georg Raphael Donner
1693–1741. Sculptor; together with Balthasar Permoser, who was active in Saxony, Donner was the most important sculptor in central Europe in the first half of the eighteenth century. Here he is shown holding a model of "Providentia". The fountain of the same name was commissioned in 1737 by the city of Vienna and unveiled in 1739 on the name day of Emperor Karl VI (Vienna, Neuer Markt; original sculptures in Lower Belvedere since 1921).

37 Carl Gustav Heraeus
1671–1725 (?). Court antiquarian; developed the imperial coin collection; co-author of the icono-graphic concept for the Karlskirche.

38 Johann Bernhard Fischer von Erlach
1656–1723. With Johann Lucas von Hildebrandt the leading architect of the Austrian Baroque. Ideal plan for Schönbrunn palace; Kollegien-kirche, Ursulinenkirche, Trinity column in Salzburg; Bohemian Court Chancery; Imperial Stables (today: Museumsquartier); Court Library; Winter Riding School. Fischer von Erlach rose to become Chief Inspector of all Court and Pleasure Buildings. Publication: *Entwurff einer historischen Architektur* (A Plan of Civil and Historical Architecture).

39 Julius Berger[69]

40 Albert Ilg
1847–96. Art historian; worked together with Rudolf Eitelberger, curator of Kunsthistorisches Museum. Author of the first monographic study on Johann Bernhard Fischer von Erlach; pro-moted neo-Baroque currents; principal author of the iconographic concept for the interior decora-tion of Kunsthistorisches Museum. Here he is depicted in conversation with the Flemish painter Seghers, thus acting as a link to the group on the extreme right and relating contemporary to historical figures.

41 Daniel Seghers
1590–1661. Flemish painter; trained under Jan Brueghel the Elder; specialised in still-lifes combining flowers and religious imagery.

42 Daniel Gran
1694–1757. Gran worked closely with Fischer von Erlach; together with Johann Michael Rottmayr he is the most important Austrian Baroque painter. Cupola frescoes in Schwarzenberg palace and Court Library, Vienna. Frescoes in the Kaisersaal of Klosterneuburg abbey, Annakirche, Vienna.

43 Sir Anthony van Dyck
1599–1641. Together with Peter Paul Rubens the foremost artist of the Flemish Baroque.

44 Rembrandt Harmenszoon van Rijn
1606–1669. The most important Dutch painter and graphic artist of the seventeenth century.

45 Isabella Clara Eugenia and Archduke
+   Albrecht VII
46
The most important rulers and art patrons of the Flemish Baroque, Isabella Clara Eugenia (1566–1633, daughter of Philip II of Spain) and Arch-duke Albrecht VII (1599–1621, brother of Emperor Rudolf II) acted jointly as governor general of the Spanish Netherlands. The couple turns here to Peter Paul Rubens, their most outstanding court artist.

47 Peter Paul Rubens
1577–1640. After a late self-portrait (c. 1638/40; KHM, Gemäldegalerie, Inv. No. 527).

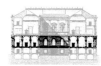

"Collection of Arms"

Collection of Arms and Armour (since 1935: Neue Burg)

*"The first part of the collections on which work was completed was the Collection of Arms. [...]
The opening was scheduled for 9 September [1889], and hence in July application was made for
employing an attendant – what a business it was can be seen from the form for provisional appointment decrees drafted by the administration office; innumerable applications were received. After the
labels and numbers for the Collection of Arms [...] were delivered it could be reported that the
installation would be completed by 1 October. [...] From 9 December the Collection of Arms was
open to the public Wednesdays and Saturdays between 10:00 a.m. and 2:00 p.m. with admission
tickets to be obtained in advance from the administration office between 10:00 a.m. and 12:00
noon. The decision to make the collection accessible before the general opening of the museum was
doubtless made taking into account the demands of tourism and the easily stimulated dissatisfaction
of certain circles, who were unhappy about the extended closure of the collections during their
transfer."*[70]

Suits of armour, bucklers or round shields, parade armour, and burgonets had by
the early Baroque period lost both their practical use and function as symbols of
status. For the construction of a new museum in the nineteenth century this collection possessed, beyond its artistic significance, an importance as a "pantheon of
Austrian-Habsburg history". This was a reception of the objects that had predominated since the age of the Baroque.[71] Thus a substantial part of the new ground floor
was reserved for the collection which was finally to be exhibited in a single location.
Up until this time various parts of the collection – body armour, court arms and
court hunt chambers, and the "Armoury of Heroes" – had been exhibited in the
Lower Belvedere palace, Ambras castle, and Laxenburg palace. They were now
arranged chronologically, but still cheek-by-jowl against a "dark red-brown" background. While the Heeresgeschichtliches Museum (Museum of Military History),
which was built 1850–56 and opened to the general public in 1869, was extensively
decorated with paintings of battle scenes, in Kunsthistorisches Museum the collection's claim to perpetuity, as well as that of its owners, was highlighted by allegorical
motifs and emblems. The grotesques are, with the exception of details, the same as
those in the other parts of the museum.
Analogous to Hall XI of the Collection of Greek and Roman Antiquities opposite,
Hall VII (formerly Hall XXVII) has a special role in the sequence of rooms. Here
pillars rather than columns support the vault, which is decorated with monumental
representations of coats of arms executed by Karl Krahl.

Collection of Arms and Armour,
former Hall XXVII, "The Age of
Karl V" (future Hall VII of the
Kunstkammer), c. 1910. Kunstverlag
Wolfrum, Inv. No. 9160 (© Kunst-
verlag Wolfrum).

Collection of Arms and Armour, former Hall XXVIII (future Hall VI of the Kunstkammer), c. 1910.
Kunstverlag Wolfrum, Inv. No. 9161 (© Kunstverlag Wolfrum).

Collection of Arms and Armour, former Hall XXV, "Arms of the Middle Ages to the Sixteenth Century" (future Hall IX of the Kunstkammer), medallions with bearing a pomegranate tree and the motto of the Order of Moderation (Friedrich III and Maximilian I). The design of the ceiling corresponds to that of the former Hall XXIX (future Hall V of the Kunstkammer) and Halls IX and XIII of the Collection of Greek and Roman Antiquities.

Collection of Arms and Armour, former Hall XXVIII, "Second Half of the Sixteenth Century" (future Hall VI of the Kunstkammer), motto of Archduke Ferdinand of Tyrol "EXCVBIAS TUETUR" ("Be Alert") and of the Duke of Burgundy and Order of the Golden Fleece "AULTRE N'AURAY".

Previous double
page: Collection
of Arms and Ar-
mour, former Hall
XXVII, "The Age
of Karl V" (future
Hall VII of the
Kunstkammer),
ceiling with coats
of arms.

Collection of Arms and
Armour in the Neue
Burg on Heldenplatz
since 1935, installation
as of 2008.

Collection of Arms and
Armour, former Hall
XXVII, "The Age of
Karl V" (future Hall VII
of the Kunstkammer),
c. 1910. Kunstverlag
Wolfrum, Inv. No. 9157
(© Kunstverlag Wolfrum).

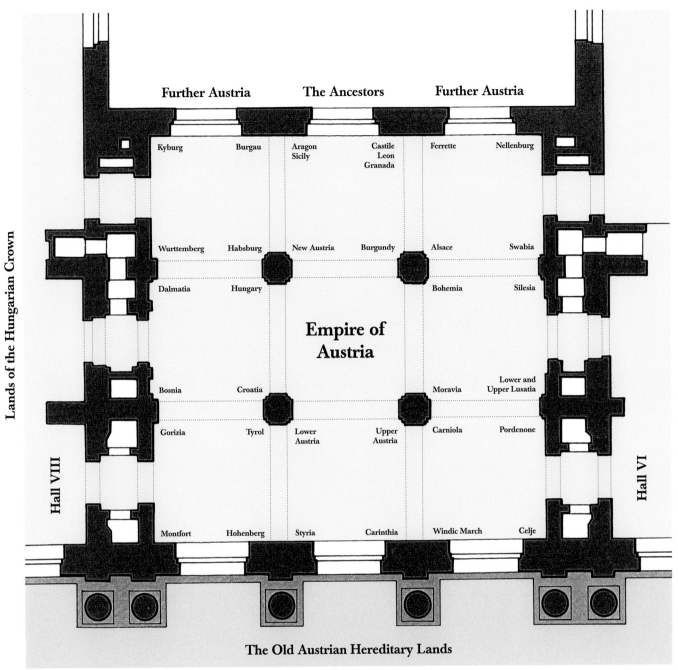

Collection of Arms and Armour, Hall VII (former Hall XXVII), scheme of ceiling decoration.

Collection of Arms and Armour, former Hall XXVII, "Age of Karl V" (future Hall VII of the Kunstkammer), ceiling with coat of arms of the Empire of Austria.

Picture Gallery, view from the cupola hall through Hall VII to Cabinet 9.

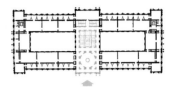

"Picture Gallery"

The design of a gallery intended for the exhibition of paintings looms large in the specialized literature of the period, as it does in Hasenauer's writings and Semper's expertise, despite the envisaged restraint of decoration. Practical, technical aspects were analysed: the area required for hanging paintings, which was to be determined as precisely as possible, the best light conditions for different types of pictures, clarity of floor plan for visitors and attendants, and adequate areas for relaxation. The separate "salons" with adjacent loggias that Hasenauer had originally planned were eliminated from the design elaborated in cooperation with Semper. The latter wished to see the space used for paintings, while visitors could equally pause to rest in the galleries. Although as early as the 1850s gas lighting had been installed to supplement illumination provided by skylights in the picture galleries at the newly constructed South Kensington Museum (1852, London, today the Victoria and Albert Museum), and electrical lighting had made considerable advances by the 1890s, Vienna carried on with natural lighting.[72]

The large galleries were each equipped with a skylight and windows in the cabinets which run around the interior courtyards to permit light to enter from the side. The considerable height of the galleries is not paralleled in the cabinets. As can be seen from the exterior façade, above the cabinets are situated the former Sekundärgalerie, which is also partially fitted with skylights, and the Collection of Coins and Medals. The proportions of the rooms and the construction of skylights were the decisive criteria. The "lantern solution" originally proposed by Hasenauer would have made impossible the cubic structure desired by Semper and also allowed the steel and glass construction to be visible from outside the building. Semper did not consider increasing the height of the halls for lighting purposes a serious problem. Similarly, he deemed that the technical difficulties involved in construction of a glass roof (in this case a double-leaf structure) that was open above – for example, the weight on the structure in the event of heavy snowfall – could be overcome. In this way, both construction of the Sekundärgalerie over the cabinets and of a balustrade running continuously around the building were possible.[73] In his first design (1867) for the competition Hasenauer had made provision for an especially large hall for the Rubens collection, which at the time was prominently exhibited in the Belvedere. In the proposal submitted jointly with Semper, the latter's wish for a regular and uniform sequence of rooms won the day, although this solution meant defining the galleries' height by that of the largest of the Rubens canvases (up to 5.35 metres). All that remained of Hasenauer's original plan were the elaborate picture frames, which were installed in particular in what is today Hall XI, and quickly became the object

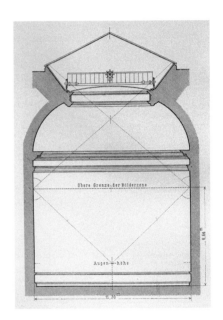

Kunsthistorisches Museum, cross section of one of the halls of the Picture Gallery. Heinrich Wagner, *Handbuch der Architektur,* part 4, vol. 6, fascicle 4: Josef Durm, Hermann Ende (eds.) *Gebäude für Sammlungen und Ausstellungen,* 2nd ed., Stuttgart, 1906, ill. 414.

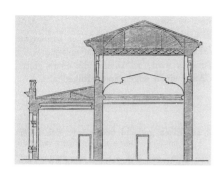

Design for a skylight. Carl Hasenauer, *Erläuternde Denkschrift über sein Project für die neu zu erbauenden k. k. Museen,* Vienna, 1867, ill. 1.

of criticism. "One could do the paintings no greater injury than by these walls of gold [...] the pictures float in a sea of gold, and of course many details are lost because of the reflection. In this way too, pictures have been brought together that simply do not belong together: the *Assumption of the Virgin Mary* [c. 1611/14; KHM, Gemäldegalerie, Inv. No. 518] which does not combine with St. Xavier [*Miracles of St. Francis Xavier,* c. 1617/18, KHM, Gemäldegalerie, Inv. No. 519] and St. Ignatius [The *Miracles of St. Ignatius,* c. 1617/18, KHM, Gemäldegalerie, Inv. No. 517]".[72] Previously, in 1878, Eduard von Engerth, who had been director of the gallery in the Belvedere since 1871, designed a number of picture frames for the new museum, whose classist tone Hasenauer later amplified with Baroque detail. Under Gustav Glück's directorship of Kunsthistorisches Museum (1911 ff.) the dissolution of this ensemble, in part, in Historic Revival style was begun. Hasenauer's creations were replaced by period frames or those made based on authentic models. In designing picture frames Hasenauer followed in the tradition of Schinkel, who had taken a great interest in this subsidiary field of interior decoration for an architect. He developed a series of frames of a more restrained character for a number of hitherto

Picture Gallery, Hall VIII c. 1910. Österreichische Nationalbibliothek, Vienna, Picture Archive, Inv. No. PCH 2179 (© Österreichische Nationalbibliothek).

Picture Gallery, Hall XIV, visible in the background are two works by Rubens in frames based on a design by Hasenauer, c. 1910. Österreichische Nationalbibliothek, Vienna, Picture Archive, Inv. No. PCH 2176 (© Österreichische National-bibliothek).

Picture Gallery, Hall I.

unframed paintings in the Berlin Gemäldegalerie (formerly Altes Museum, 1827–30).[75]

A number of designs by Hasenauer for stucco ornament and portrait medallions for the ceiling of Picture Gallery have also been preserved.[76] Many paintings were originally hung quite close to the stuccoed apophyge and thus drew the observer's gaze imperceptibly to the ceiling area. For this reason varied decorative schemes were employed. Although these schemes are used more than once, the overall formal impression is disparate. Picture frames, ornaments, reliefs and portrait medallions are, however, uniformly monochrome.

The overdoors in the galleries were decorated with yet further portrait busts mounted on inscribed pedestals, which were later removed. In the 1980s reinstallation began of these plaster busts; not all of their original locations could be determined however.[77]

Adolf Reich, "View of a Hall in the Picture Gallery", 1941. KHM Archive, Inv. No. XIX 10.

Previous double
pages: Picture
Gallery, Hall XIV,
c. 1916.

Gemäldegalerie,
Cabinet 3, view
from Hall VII to
Cabinet 9.

Overleaf,
double page:
Picture Gallery,
Hall XI, overdoors
with busts of
artists and ceiling
apophyge with
skylight.

Picture Gallery,
Halls I and II
overdoors with
busts of artists.

Picture Gallery, artists' busts in the overdoors of the Picture Gallery (Viktor Tilgner).

SAAL XI

Picture Gallery,
Hall XI, stucco
decoration in ceiling
apophyge.

Picture Gallery, Hall XI, stucco decoration in ceiling apophyge, portrait medallion of Gerhard Terborch (1617–81).

Picture Gallery,
Hall XV, war
damage, 1945.

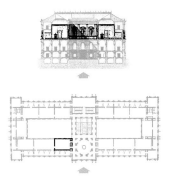

Picture Gallery, Hall XV
in 2008.

"Coins and Medals"

The Coin Cabinet

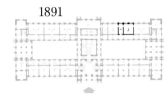

1891

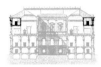

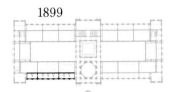

1899

The use of skylights to illuminate the Picture Gallery halls should have excluded construction of a story above. However, as the cabinets running around the halls were lower in height, it was possible to include another story, which nonetheless offered considerably less floor space. The only deviation from this plan was what is today known as the Bassano Hall, located not above one of the lower cabinets of the Picture Gallery, but above Hall VIII which is of the same height as the cabinets. The absence of a skylight was compensated by large windows facing Babenbergerstrasse. Today these windows are concealed by wall panelling necessary for technical reasons. Originally the "Copir-Säle", restoration facilities, and collections of water-colours, drawings, studies and sketches were accommodated on the second floor. This collection was for the most part divided up among other museums (Albertina and Belvedere) in the 1920s.

At the time the museum opened the Coin Cabinet was still part of the Collection of Greek and Roman Antiquities, and was exhibited in what are today Halls XV and XVI on the ground floor. In 1899 the two collections were separated, and the coins have since been displayed on the second floor. In the three halls of the Collection of Coins and Medals, the original fittings have been preserved to a great extent. Lectern and wall display cases, frames for the portrait collection of Archduke Ferdinand of Tyrol, intrados of the doors, and delicate decoration of the ceiling (into which skylights were subsequently installed) have all been carefully matched with one another. Whilst historic exhibition display and technology have been preserved in part throughout the collections on the ground floor, here they can be seen in concentrated form and virtually unaltered.

Until its closure in the 1990s, the Sekundärgalerie occupied the series of rooms between cupola and Bassano Halls opposite the Collection of Coins and Medals. The restoration ateliers had been moved even earlier to non-public areas of the museum, and the operation of the "Copir-Saal" discontinued.

Coin Cabinet, Hall I.

Coin Cabinet, Hall I,
original lectern display
cases and portrait col-
lection of Archduke
Ferdinand II of Tyrol.

Overleaf, double page: Median risalit on Maria-Theresien-Platz, attic, cupola and lanterns. The inscription reads, "Den Denkmälern der Kunst und des Alterthums Kaiser Franz Joseph I. MDCCCLXXXI" ("For the Monuments of Art and Antiquity Emperor Franz Josef I MDCCCLXXXI").

Coin Cabinet, Hall I, original lectern display cases.

DEN DENKMÆLERN DER
KAISER F
MDC

ST UND DES ALTERTHUMS
Z JOSEPH I.
XXXI.

1 Krzysztof Pomian, *Der Ursprung des Museums. Vom Sammeln*, Berlin, 1998.

2 See in general: Peter Böttger, *Die Alte Pinakothek in München. Architektur, Ausstattung und malerisches Programm (Studien zur Kunst des 19. Jahrhunderts*, 15), Munich, 1972, pp. 49 ff.

3 See in general: Kurt Mollik, Hermann Reining, Rudolf Wurzer, *Planung und Verwirklichung der Wiener Ringstraßenzone* (Renate Wagner-Rieger [ed.], *Die Wiener Ringstraße. Bild einer Epoche* III [illustrations]), Wiesbaden, 1980.

4 *Beschreibung und Grundriss der Haupt- und Residenzstadt Wien*, Vienna, 1802, p. 9, cited after Mollik, Reining, Wurzer, 1980 (quoted note 3), p. 35.

5 *Die Votivkirche in Wien. Denkschrift des Baucomités*, Vienna, 1879, p. 2.

6 *Wiener Zeitung*, 25 December 1857, cited in Mollik, Reining, Wurzer 1980 (quoted note 3), pp. 113 f.

7 See Mollik, Reining, Wurzer 1980 (quoted note 3), pp. 355 ff.

8 See Alphons Lhotsky, *Festschrift des Kunsthistorischen Museums in Wien, 1891–1941,* part 1 *Die Baugeschichte der Museen und der Neuen Burg,* Vienna, 1941; part 2: *Die Geschichte der Sammlungen, 2. Hälfte. Von Maria Theresia bis zum Ende der Monarchie,* Vienna, 1941–45. Cited here: Part 1, pp. 36 f.

9 Lhotsky 1941 (quoted note 8), pp. 44 f.

10 See in general: Harry Francis Mallgrave, *Gottfried Semper. Architect of the Nineteenth Century,* London, 1996; Winfried Nerdinger and Werner Oechslin, *Gottfried Semper 1803–1879,* Exh. Cat. Architekturmuseum, Munich, 2003, Museum für Gestaltung, Zurich, 2003/04; Rainald Franz and Andreas Nierhaus (eds.), *Gottfried Semper und Wien. Die Wirkung des Architekten auf "Wissenschaft, Industrie und Kunst",* Vienna, 2007.

11 See in general: Ulrike Planner-Steiner and Klaus Eggert, *Friedrich von Schmidt. Gottfried Semper. Carl von Hasenauer* (Renate Wagner-Rieger [ed.], *Die Wiener Ringstraße. Bild einer Epoche,* vol. 8), Wiesbaden 1978; Richard Kurdiovsky, "Die Zeichnungen Carl Hasenauers in der Wiener Albertina", in: Rainald Franz and Andreas Nierhaus (eds.), *Gottfried Semper und Wien.*

Die Wirkung des Architekten auf "Wissenschaft, Industrie und Kunst", Vienna, 2007, pp. 143 ff.

12 Carl Hasenauer, *Erläuternde Denkschrift über sein Project für die neu zu erbauenden k. k. Museen,* Vienna, 1867.

13 Expertise, Semper Archives, ETH Zurich.

14 Cited in: *Die k. k. Hofmuseen in Wien und Gottfried Semper. Drei Denkschriften Gottfried Semper's herausgegeben von seinen Söhnen,* Innsbruck, 1892.

15 Born Copenhagen 1813, died Vienna, 1891; selected works: Heeresgeschichtliches Museum, Arsenal, 1856; Musikverein 1867–70; Stock Exchange 1874–77; Reichsrat (today: Parliament) 1874–83.

16 Born Vienna 1828, died Vienna, 1883; selected works: Votivkirche 1856–79; Museum for Art and Industry (today: Museum for Applied Arts) 1871; University 1883.

17 Born Berlin 1810, died Vienna, 1874; director of the building office for the Empress Elisabeth Western Railway 1856.

18 Theophil Hansen, "*Erläuterungen zu dem von dem Unterzeichneten verfaßten Projekte der zwischen dem Burgthore und k. k. Hofstallgebäuden neu auszuführenden k. k. Museen in Wien",* 31. 3. 1867, in: *Allgemeine Bauzeitung,* 32, 1867, pp. 306 ff., cited in: Lhotsky 1941-45 (quoted note 8), p. 49.

19 Hasenauer 1867 (quoted note 12), pp. 11 ff.

20 Rudolf Eitelberger von Edelberg, *Denkschrift über den Bau und die Organisation des Museums für Kunst in Wien,* Vienna, 1867.

21 See Peter Noever (ed.), *Gottfried Semper. The Ideal Museum. Practical Art in Metals and Hard Materials,* Vienna, 2007.

22 Manfred Semper, *Hasenauer und Semper. Eine Erwiderung und Richtigstellung,* Hamburg,1895.

23 Gottfried Semper, "Bericht, die Prüfung und Vergleichung zweier Projecte für den Bau der neuen k. k. Museen in Wien betreffend", in: Semper, *Schriften,* 1892 (quoted note 14), pp. 3 ff.

24 Quoted according to Semper 1895 (quoted note 22), p. 7.

25 Idem

26 See Christoph Hölz, "Semper und Wien 1869–1879", in: Winfried Nerdinger and Werner Oechslin, *Gottfried Semper*

1803–1879, Exh. Cat. Architekturmuseum, Munich, 2003 – Museum für Gestaltung, Zurich 2003/04, pp. 433 ff. On relations between Semper, Wagner and Nietzsche, see the recently published study by Heidrun Laudel, "Das Bekleidungsprinzip – Sempers künstlerisches Credo", in: Rainald Franz and Andreas Nierhaus (eds.), *Gottfried Semper und Wien. Die Wirkung des Architekten auf "Wissenschaft, Industrie und Kunst",* Vienna, 2007, pp. 17 ff.

27 Emperor Franz Josef I to Minister of the Interior Taaffe, 17. 7. 1870, cited by Margaret Gottfried in *Das Wiener Kaiserforum. Utopien zwischen Hofburg und Museumsquartier,* Vienna, 2001, p. 81.

28 Gottfried Semper, Ueber Baustyle. Ein Vortrag gehalten auf dem Rathaus in Zürich am 4. März 1869, Zurich, 1869, p. 28.

29 The term "(imperial) forum" originated in imperial Rome and designated large ceremonial plazas which might be the location for porticos, temples, market halls, basilicas, and libraries. Laid out on a symmetrical plan they were the pinnacle of imperial representation in Roman cities.

30 Cited in: Eduard Irmisch, *Beitrag zur Baugeschichte der Neuen Hofburg,* Vienna 1932, pp. 19, 13 f.

31 Irmisch 1932 (quoted note 30), p. 17.

32 Ludwig Baumann, Allgemeines Bauprogramm, January 1906. Allgemeines Verwaltungsarchiv (AVA), Ministry of the Interior, Wiener Stadterweiterungsfonds, Burgbaukommission 91.

33 Lhotsky 1941 (quoted note 8), p. 145.

34 Irmisch 1932 (quoted note 30), p. 24.

35 Irmisch 1932 (quoted note 30), p. 25.

36 Gottfried Semper, "Entwurf eines Programmes für die bildnerische Decoration der Façaden des k. k. Museums für Kunst und Alterthum", in: Semper, *Schriften,* 1892 (quoted note 14), pp. 51 ff.

37 The Semper's original designations have been maintained here.

38 The author is indebted to the artist's great grandson Mr. Wolfgang Tautenhayn, Vienna, for this information.

39 Semper 1892 (quoted note 14), p. 63.

40 Carl von Lützow, "Das Kunsthistorische Hofmuseum in Wien", in: *Zeitschrift für Bildende Kunst,* N. S. III, 1891, p. 99.

41 Böttger 1972 (quoted note 2).

42 Semper 1892 (quoted note 14), p. 19.

43 According to another interpretation, the visitor ascending the staircase strides toward the "aesthetic illumination" that conquers "passions"; see Beat Wyss, "Habsburgs Panorama. Zur Ikonologie und 'Psychoanalyse' der Wiener Museumsbauten", in: Gabriele Helke (ed.), *100 Jahre Kunsthistorisches Museum. Das Kunsthistorische Museum als Denkmal und Gesamtkunstwerk (Jahrbuch der Kunsthistorischen Sammlungen in Wien,* 88 [N. F.

vol. 52]), 1992, pp. 125 ff. In this connection, the analogous subject matter of a number of the medallions of the façade may also be recalled.

44 Albert Ilg, *Zwickelbilder im Stiegenhause des k. k. Kunsthistorischen Hof-Museums zu Wien, von Ernst und Gustav Klimt und Franz Matsch,* Vienna, 1893, p. 1.

45 For general background, see Werner Kitlitschka, *Die Malerei der Wiener Ringstraße* (Renate Wagner-Rieger [ed.], *Die Wiener Ringstraße. Bild einer Epoche,* vol. 10), Wiesbaden, 1981; Agnes Husslein-Arco and Alfred Weidinger (eds.), *Gustav Klimt und die Künstler-Compagnie* Exh. Cat. Belvedere, Vienna, 2007.

46 Ilg 1893 (quoted note 44).

47 Ibid.

48 The sequence and designation of the themes correspond to those used by Albert Ilg in the work cited above (1893, quoted note 44).

49 See Vinzenz Oberhammer, "Michael v. Munkácsys Deckengemälde im Stiegenhaus des Kunsthistorischen Museums in Wien", in: *Jahrbuch der kunsthistorischen Sammlungen in Wien,* vol. 70, 1974, pp. 221-317.

50 The coat of arms does not correspond to the generally accepted identification of the pope as Julius II (della Rovere).

51 Thomas W. Gaethgens, *Die Berliner Museumsinsel im Deutschen Kaiserreich,* Munich,1992, p. 72.

52 Mayor of Menat Khufu, Overseer of the Eastern Desert, middle of the Twelfth Dynasty, c. 1870 B.C. The main room is of a square configuration, 9.60 – 9.70 metres; height 5.89 metres.

53 Richard Lepsius, *Denkmäler aus Ägypten und Äthiopien,* Berlin, 1849.

54 See Seipel (ed.), *Ägyptomanie. Ägypten in der europäischen Kunst 1730–1930,* Exh. Cat. Künstlerhaus, Vienna, 1994.

55 See Michaela Hüttner, "Papyrusbündelsäulen in Wien", in: *Timelines. Studies in Honour of Manfred Bietak,* vol. 1, Paris, 2006, pp. 151–55.

56 Johann Joachim Winckelmann, *Geschichte der Kunst des Altertums,* Vienna, 1776.

57 Albert Ilg, in: Beatrix Kriller and Georg Kugler, *Das Kunsthistorische Museum. Die Architektur und Ausstattung,* Vienna, 1991, p. 11.

58 AVA (see quoted note 32), Stadterweiterung, Fasz. 44, 21058, Accord-Protocoll, 25 May 1890, cited in Kriller and Kugler 1991 (quoted note 57), p. 163.

59 Fillitz does not provide a conclusive identification; see Hermann Fillitz, *Das Deckengemälde im Hochparterre-Mittelsaal des Kunsthistorischen Museums,* Vienna, n.d.

60 Ibid.

61 Ibid.

62 Ibid.

63 Ibid: Burgkmair; Kriller and Kugler, 1991 (quoted note 57), p. 174: Springinklee.

64 Fillitz, n.d. (quoted note 59): Stabius (?); Kriller and Kugler 1991 (quoted note 57), p. 174: Stabius.

65 Fillitz, n.d. (quoted note 59): Marx Treitzsauerwein (?); Kriller and Kugler 1991 (quoted note 57), p. 163: Colin.

66 Fillitz, n.d. (quoted note 59): Seusenhofer (?); Kriller and Kugler 1991 (quoted note 57), p. 163: Burgkmair.

67 Fillitz, n.d. (quoted note 59).

68 Ibid.

69 Ibid., Jacques Callot (?), French etcher, 1592–1635.

70 Lhotsky [1941–1945] (quoted note 8), p. 615.

71 Christian Beaufort and Matthias Pfaffenbichler, *Meisterwerke der Hofjagd- und Rüstkammer (Kurzführer durch das Kunsthistorische Museum,* ed. Wilfried Seipel, vol. 3), Vienna, 2005, p. 13.

72 "Artificial lighting of museums […] has up until now [1906] rarely been introduced, and mainly in such collections which are to be open in the evening to accommodate the class of the population who have to spend the entire day at work", Heinrich Wagner, *Handbuch der Architektur,* part 4, vol. 6, fascicle 4: Josef Durm, Hermann Ende (eds.) *Gebäude für Sammlungen und Ausstellungen,* 2nd ed., Stuttgart, 1906, p. 314.

73 See Semper, 1892 (quoted note 14), pp. 10 f.

74 Ernst Klarwill, *Wie man die Wiener Galerie verdorben hat. Ein Beitrag zur Geschichte des kunsthistorischen Hofmuseums,* Vienna, 1892, pp. 9 f.

75 Bettina von Roenne (ed.), *Ein Architekt rahmt Bilder. Karl Friedrich Schinkel und die Berliner Gemäldegalerie,* Exh. Cat. Staatliche Museen zu Berlin, Gemäldegalerie, Berlin, 2007.

76 Dated 1882; Vienna, Albertina; illustration in Kriller-Kugler 1991 (quoted note 57), pp. 274 f.

77 The following list of portrait busts of artists by Tilger refers to the original arrangement according to Lhotsky 1941 (quoted note 8), pp. 170 f. The hall numbers are those currently in use. I: Busts: Barthel Beham, Bartholomäus Bruyn the Elder, Adam Elsheimer; II: Busts: Hans Holbein the Elder, Hans Suess von Kulmbach, Bernhard Strigel; Portraits: Christian Seybold, Jan Kupetzky, Francesco Casanova, Martin Johann Schmidt, known as Kremser Schmidt, Jacob van Schuppen, Daniel Gran, Martin van Meytens, Paul Troger, Franz Anton Maulpertsch, Martin Knoller, Victorias; III: Busts: Hans Mielich, Hans Rottenhammer, Hans von Aachen, Bartholomäus Spranger; IV: Busts: Paolo Veronese, Domenico Robustio named Tintoretto, Diego Velázquez; Portraits: Benvenuto Tisi known as Il Garofalo, Giulio Romano, Alessandro Bonvicino known as Moretto da Brescia, Andrea del Sarto, Andrea Meldolla named Schiavone, Annibale Carracci, Giovanni Antonio Bassi named Il Sodoma, Guido Reni, Bartolomé Esteban Murillo, Jusepe de Ribera; V: Busts: Leonardo da Vinci, Raphael, Michelangelo; Portraits: Domenico Fetti, Sebastiano del Piombo, Francesco Bassano, Francesco Bec-caruzzi, Giovanni Francesco Barbieri named Guercino, Giambattista Tiepolo, Luca Giordano, Salvator Rosa, Stefano (?) Zampieri, Michelangelo Merisi named Caravaggio; VI: Busts: Giovanni Bellini, Palma Vecchio, Giorgio da Caselfranco gen. Giorgione, Titian; Portraits: Antonello da Messina, Andrea da Murano, Antonio Vivarini, Vittore Carpaccio, Francesco Perugino, Marco Basaiti, Correggio, Francesco Francia, Fra Bartolomeo, Bonifazio Veneziano, Paris Bordone, Vincenzo Catena; VII: Busts: Benozzo Gozzoli, Andrea Mantegna, Cima da Conegliano, Luca Signorelli; Schrifttafeln: Piero di Cosimo, Tommaso da Modena, Lorenzo Costa, F. P. da Pistoia, Giuliano Bugiardini, Francesco Morandini, Giovanni Mansueti, Sebastiano Florigerio, Dosso Dossi, Lodovico Mazzolino; VIII: Busts in original location with inscription: Hans Burgkmair the Elder, Lucas Cranach the Elder, Albrecht Dürer; IX: Busts: Martin Schongauer, Albrecht Altdorfer, Hans Baldung named Grien; Portraits: Johann Michael Rottmayr, Joseph Roos, Martino Altomonte, Anton Faistenberger; X: Busts: Frans Hals, Salomon van Ruysdael, Adriaen van de Velde; Portraits: Cornelis van Poelenburgh, Jan van Huysum, Wilhelm Schubert von Ehrenberg, Adam Pynacker, Gottfried Kneller, Gerard de Lairesse, Jan van der Heyden, Cornelis (?) Saftleven, Egbert van der Poel, Pieter de Molijn; XI: Busts: David Teniers d. J., Jan Steen, Aelbert Cuyp, Adriaen van Ostade; Portraits: Jacob van der Does, Dirck van Bergen, Ludolf Backhuyzen, Allart van Everdingen, Gerard ter Borch, Meindert Hobbema, Jan van de Capelle, Nicolaes Berchem, Justus van Egmont, Franz de Hamilton; XII: Busts: Peter Paul Rubens, Pieter Bruegel, Frans Snyders; Portraits: Frans Snyders, Philips Wouwerman, Christoph Paudiss, Simon de Vlieger, Theodor van Thulden, Jacob Jordaens, Gaspar de Crayer, Jaques d'Arthois, Gonzales Coques, Pieter Verelst; XIII: Busts: Bartolomeus van der Helst, Anthony van Dyck, Rembrandt Harmenszoon van Rijn; Portraits: Abraham Brouwer, Peeter Neefs d. J., Michiel Jansz van Mierevelt, Jan van Goyen, Jan (?) van den Hoecke, Gabriel Metsu, Frans II. Francken, Joos de Momper, Hendrick van Balen, Otto van Veen; XIV: Busts: Gerard David, Hans Memling, Jan Brueghel the Elder (?), Bernaert van Orley; Portraits: Martin van Cleve, Martin de Vos, Michiel Coxcie, Jacob Cornelisz van Oostsanen, Jan van Scorel, Roelant Savery, Frans Floris, Pieter Aertsen, Lucas I. (?) van Valckenborch, Pieter Pourbus, Anthonis Mor, Marinus van Reymerswaele; Reliefs: Portrait Painting, Madonnas of the Cult of Saints, Architectural Painting, Still Life, Animal Portrayals, Genre Painting; XV: Busts: Jan van Eyck, Lucas van Leyden, Jan Cornelisz Vermeyen; Portraits: Jan Mostaert, Jan Gossaert named Mabuse, Quinten Massys, Maerten van Heemskerck, Herri met de Bles, Joachim Patinier, Hieronymus Bosch, Jan Sanders van Hemessen, Rogier van der Weyden, Geertgen tot Sint Jans.

Overleaf, double page: Ground floor, ambulatory with Roman portrait busts.

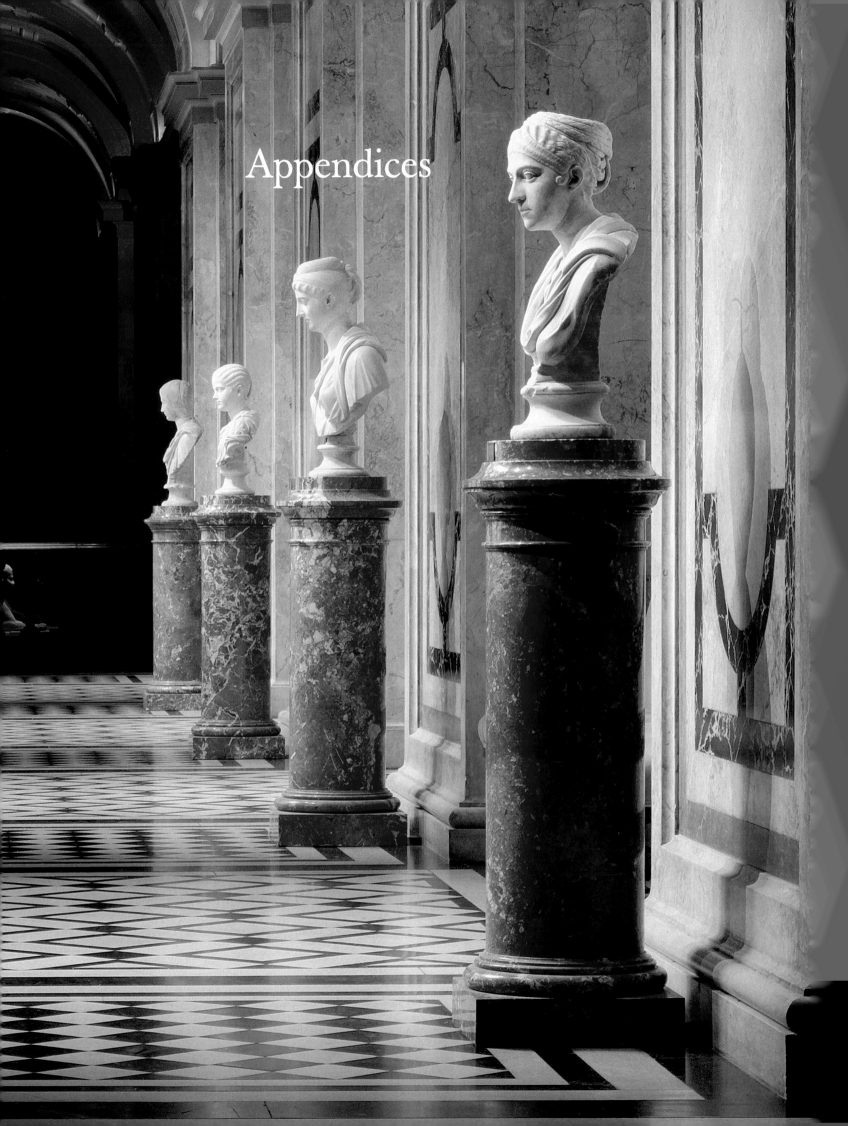

Appendices

Materials

Façades

Foundation walls:
Sarmatischer limestone from Atzgersdorf

Base:
Oslip stone (hard yellow calcitic lime)

Facing to the first floor:
Zogelsdorf stone (calcitic sandstone), Trento

Facing above first floor:
Stone from Mannersdorf, Mokritz (tabernacle), Bruck, Vinicia, Aflenz, Medulin, Merlera, Sutno

Roof:
originally red and blue slate from southern France and England

Interior

All floors in vestibules and corridors:
Carrara II, ornaments in black Belgian limestone ("Noir de Belgique", Mazy, Namur)

Staircase, massive stairs, balustrades, most floors in vestibules and corridors:
Carrara II
Balusters: *dark red Engelsberg marble*
Columns: *Grand' Antique (Pyrenees), Porto Venere (black with golden yellow, veins), Baveno, Diorite, Karlskrona etc.*

Cupola hall
Balusters: *dark red Engelsberg marble*;
pillars, *artificial marble, in the foreground columns of Porto Venere*

Picture Gallery:
base facing of black Belgian limestone

Stairs to second floor:
marble from Kainach valley, Styria

Galleries on ground floor:

I (Egyptian and Near Eastern Collection) and V (Egyptian and Near Eastern Collection), *Aswan granite from (rose-coloured granite)*

VII (Egyptian and Near Eastern Collection), XIV (Greek and Roman Antiquities), XX (Kunstkammer XII), XXIV (Kunstkammer X), XXXVI (Kunstkammer I), XXXII (Kunstkammer III): supporting column, *Granite from Baveno;* base plates and capitals, *Untersberg and Pörtschach marble*

IV (Egyptian and Near Eastern Collection), VIII (Greek and Roman Antiquities), XV (Greek and Roman Antiquities), XVII (Greek and Roman Antiquities), XXX (Kunstkammer IV): supporting column, *diorite from the Fichtelgebirge region;* base plates and capitals, *Pörtschach marble*

X (Greek and Roman Antiquities): supporting column, *granite from Karlskrona;* base plates and capitals, *Carrara II*
Pilasters and walls, *artificial marble ("red granite");* floors, *white Carrara and red "rouge griotte"* also the piers of Halls XII (Greek and Roman Antiquities), XXVIII (Greek and Roman Antiquities) in addition to true columns, XXIX (Kunstkammer V)

XI (Greek and Roman Antiquities): piers, *yellow artificial marble (imitation giallo antico)*
Niche columns: *artificial marble ("violet-grey ophicalcite from Pfons")*

XII (Greek and Roman Antiquities), XXII (Greek and Roman Antiquities): *blue-grey granite from Mauthausen,* base plates; *Untersberg marble*

XXVII (Kunstkammer VII): *grey imitation granite*; niches – columns: *artificial marble ("violet-grey ophicalcite from Pfons")*

Source: Alois Kieslinger, *Die Steine der Wiener Ringstraße. Ihre technische und künstlerische Bedeutung* (*Die Wiener Ringstraße. Bild einer Epoche*, vol. 4), Wiesbaden, 1972, p. 249 ff.

Imitation Marble – Stucco Lustro

The basic material for the production of artificial marble is gypsum alabaster, to which glue is added in order to prolong the drying process of the plaster. To attain a smooth finished surface without cracks requires the use of base surfaces which do not expand or contract, for example, brick columns or inexpensive natural stone. The mixture of plaster and glue was formerly generally coloured with marble powder. The mass thus produced could be given the desired structure by repeated kneading, pulling and the admixture of various coloured powders, etc. Differently than stucco lustro, artificial marble is coloured throughout. In stucco lustro a marbled effect is achieved by painting the wet lime mortar *al fresco*. The kneaded mass of artificial marble was then spread on a brick board, or tabletop covered with jute (both methods promote dehydration), further structured, and only then applied to the final base surface. The mass requires eight days to dry completely. Following several smoothing procedures and after the mass had dried completely, it was given a final polish using beeswax. Notwithstanding the complicated production process, artificial marble is both far less costly and lighter than true marble. These are considerable advantages even though the coloured gypsum mortar of course is not endowed with the resiliency to shock of natural stone. When mastery of the production technique is as consummate as in the two imperial museums, it is difficult to distinguish between natural and artificial stone, other than by the absent grouting, which may however also be simulated. Imitation marble is also relatively warm, whilst natural stone is cold to the touch. Undisputed master of the *métier* was Anton Detoma, *k. u. k. Hofkunstmarmorierer und Stukkateur* (Imperial and Royal Court Artificial Marble and Stucco Artisan). After training in Munich and working in Stockholm and Berlin, Detoma moved to Vienna in 1865 at Heinrich Ferstel's invitation. Here he oversaw a flourishing business until his death in 1895.

From Alois Kieslinger, *Die Steine der Wiener Ringstraße. Ihre technische und künstlerische Bedeutung* (Die Wiener Ringstraße. Bild einer Epoche, vol. 4), Wiesbaden, 1972, p. 119 ff.

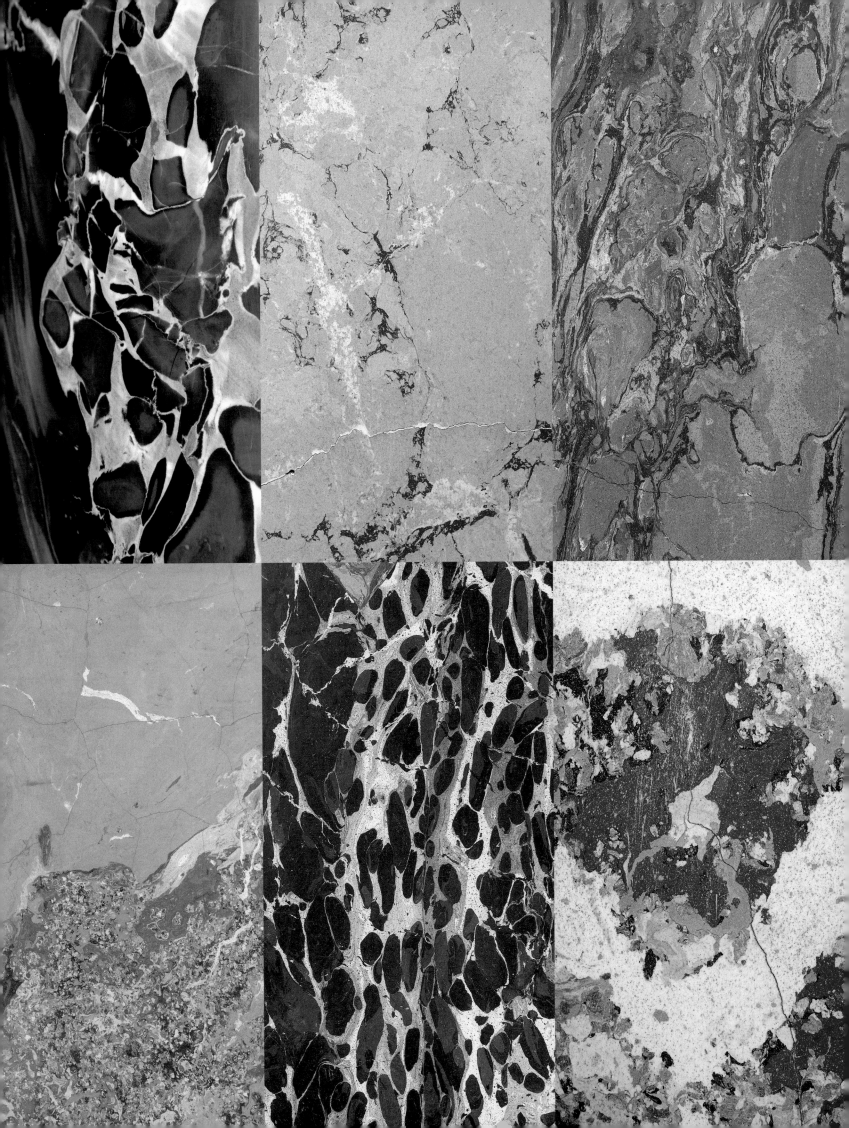

Bibliography

Exh. Cat. Bettina von Roenne (ed.), *Ein Architekt rahmt Bilder. Karl Friedrich Schinkel und die Berliner Gemäldegalerie,* Berlin (Staatliche Museen zu Berlin, Gemäldegalerie), 2007.

Exh. Cat. Winfried Nerdinger (ed.), *Leo von Klenze. Architekt zwischen Kunst und Hof 1784–1864,* Munich (Architekturmuseum), 2000.

Exh. Cat. Winfried Nerdinger and Werner Oechslin, *Gottfried Semper 1803–1879,* Munich (Architekturmuseum) 2003 – Zurich (Museum für Gestaltung), 2003/04.

Exh. Cat. Wilfried Seipel (ed.), *Ägyptomanie. Ägypten in der europäischen Kunst 1730–1930,* Vienna (Künstlerhaus), 1994.

Exh. Cat. Hermann Fillitz (ed.), *Der Traum vom Glück. Das Phänomen des europäischen Historismus,* Vienna (Künstlerhaus and Akademie der Bildenden Künste), 1996.

Exh. Cat. *Das ungebaute Wien. Projekte für die Metropole 1800 bis 2000,* Vienna (Historisches Museum der Stadt Wien), 1999.

Exh. Cat. Agnes Husslein-Arco and Alfred Weidinger (eds.), *Gustav Klimt und die Künstler-Compagnie,* Vienna (Belvedere), 2007.

Christian Beaufort and Matthias Pfaffenbichler, *Meisterwerke der Hofjagd- und Rüstkammer* (Kurzführer durch das Kunsthistorische Museum, ed. by Wilfried Seipel, vol. 3), Vienna, 2005.

Beschreibung und Grundriss der Haupt- und Residenzstadt Wien, Vienna, 1802.

Cäcilia Bischoff, *Ludwig Baumann (1853–1936) Architekt in Wien. Stilpluralismus als ökonomische Strategie,* dissertation, University of Bonn, 2003.

Peter Böttger, *Die Alte Pinakothek in München. Architektur, Ausstattung und malerisches Programm* (Studien zur Kunst des 19. Jahrhunderts, Vol. 15), Munich, 1972.

Rudolf Eitelberger von Edelberg, *Denkschrift über den Bau und die Organisation des Museums für Kunst in Wien,* Vienna, 1867.

Hermann Fillitz, *Das Deckengemälde im Hochparterre-Mittelsaal des Kunsthistorischen Museums,* Vienna, n.d.

Rainald Franz and Andreas Nierhaus (eds.), *Gottfried Semper und Wien. Die Wirkung des Architekten auf "Wissenschaft, Industrie und Kunst",* Vienna, 2007.

Detail of the portal in the median risalit on Maria Theresien-Platz, spandrel (David).

Thomas W. Gaethgens, *Die Berliner Museumsinsel im Deutschen Kaiserreich,* Munich, 1992.

Margaret Gottfried, *Das Wiener Kaiserforum. Utopien zwischen Hofburg und Museumsquartier,* Vienna, 2001.

Theophil Hansen, *Erläuterungen zu dem von dem Unterzeichneten verfaßten Projekte der zwischen dem Burgthore und k. k. Hofstallgebäuden neu auszuführenden k. k. Museen in Wien, 31.3.1867* in: *Allgemeine Bauzeitung,* 32, 1867.

Elke Harten, *Museen und Museumsprojekte der Französischen Revolution. Ein Beitrag zur Entstehungsgeschichte einer Institution,* Münster, 1989.

Carl Hasenauer, *Erläuternde Denkschrift über sein Project für die neu zu erbauenden k. k. Museen,* Vienna, 1867.

Herbert Haupt, *Das Kunsthistorische Museum. Die Geschichte des Hauses am Ring. Hundert Jahre im Spiegel historischer Ereignisse,* Vienna, 1991.

Gabriele Helke (ed.), *100 Jahre Kunsthistorisches Museum. Das Kunsthistorische Museum als Denkmal und Gesamtkunstwerk* (Jahrbuch der kunsthistorischen Sammlungen in Wien, Vol. 88 [N. S. vol. 52]), 1992.

Christoph Hölz, "Semper und Wien 1869–1879", in: Exh. Cat. Winfried Nerdinger and Werner Oechslin, *Gottfried Semper 1803–1879,* Munich (Architekturmuseum), 2003, Zurich (Museum für Gestaltung), 2003/04.

Albert Ilg, *Zwickelbilder im Stiegenhause des k. k. Kunsthistorischen Hof-Museums zu Wien, von Ernst und Gustav Klimt und Franz Matsch,* Vienna, 1893.

"Ihm, welcher der Andacht Tempel baut …" Ludwig I. und die Alte Pinakothek. Festschrift zum Jubiläumsjahr 1986, Munich, 1986.

Eduard Irmisch, *Beitrag zur Baugeschichte der Neuen Hofburg,* Vienna, 1932.

Werner Kitlitschka, *Die Malerei der Wiener Ringstraße* (Renate Wagner-Rieger [ed.], Die Wiener Ringstraße. Bild einer Epoche, Vol. X), Wiesbaden, 1981.

Ernst Klarwill, *Wie man die Wiener Galerie verdorben hat. Ein Beitrag zur Geschichte des kunsthistorischen Hofmuseums,* Vienna, 1892.

Beatrix Kriller and Georg Kugler, *Das Kunsthistorische Museum. Die Architektur und Ausstattung,* Vienna, 1991.

Richard Kurdiovsky, "Die Zeichnungen Carl Hasenauers in der Wiener Albertina", in: Rainald Franz and Andreas Nierhaus (eds.), *Gottfried Semper und Wien. Die Wirkung des Architekten auf „Wissenschaft, Industrie und Kunst"*, Vienna, 2007.

Heidrun Laudel, *Gottfried Semper. Architektur und Stil,* Dresden, 1991.

Heidrun Laudel, "Das Bekleidungsprinzip – Sempers künstlerisches Credo", in: Rainald Franz – Andreas Nierhaus (eds.), *Gottfried Semper und Wien. Die Wirkung des Architekten auf „Wissenschaft, Industrie und Kunst"*, Vienna, 2007.

Richard Lepsius, *Denkmäler aus Ägypten und Äthiopien,* Berlin, 1849.

Alphons Lhotsky, *Festschrift des Kunsthistorischen Museums in Wien, 1891–1941. Erster Teil. Die Baugeschichte der Museen und der Neuen Burg,* Vienna, 1941; *Zweiter Teil. Die Geschichte der Sammlungen, 2. Hälfte. Von Maria Theresia bis zum Ende der Monarchie,* Vienna [1941–1945].

Carl von Lützow, "Das Kunsthistorische Hofmuseum in Wien I", in: *Zeitschrift für Bildende Kunst* N. S. III, 1891, 97–102; "II".

Harry Francis Mallgrave, *Gottfried Semper. Architect of the Nineteenth Century,* London, 1996.

Kurt Mollik, Hermann Reining, and Rudolf Wurzer, *Planung und Verwirklichung der Wiener Ringstraßenzone* (Renate Wagner-Rieger [ed.], Die Wiener Ringstraße. Bild einer Epoche, Vol. III, Texts), Wiesbaden, 1980.

Peter Noever (ed.), *Gottfried Semper. The Ideal Museum. Practical Art in Metals and Hard Materials,* Vienna, 2007.

Vinzenz Oberhammer, "Michael v. Munkácsys Deckengemälde im Stiegenhaus des Kunsthistorischen Museums in Wien", in: *Jahrbuch der kunsthistorischen Sammlungen in Wien,* vol. 70, 1974.

Ulrike Planner-Steiner and Klaus Eggert, *Friedrich von Schmidt. Gottfried Semper. Carl von Hasenauer* (Renate Wagner-Rieger [ed.], Die Wiener Ringstraße. Bild einer Epoche, Vol. VIII), Wiesbaden, 1978.

Krzysztof Pomian, *Der Ursprung des Museums. Vom Sammeln,* Berlin, 1998.

Gottfried Semper, *Ueber Baustyle. Ein Vortrag gehalten auf dem Rathaus in Zürich am 4. März 1869,* Zurich, 1869.

Die k. k. Hofmuseen in Wien und Gottfried Semper. Drei Denkschriften Gottfried Semper's herausgegeben von seinen Söhnen, Innsbruck, 1892.

Gottfried Semper, "Bericht, die Prüfung und Verglei- chung zweier Projecte für den Bau der neuen k. k. Museen in Wien betreffend", in: *Die k. k. Hofmuseen in Wien und Gottfried Semper.* Drei Denkschriften Gottfried Semper's herausgegeben von seinen Söhnen, Innsbruck, 1892.

Gottfried Semper, "Entwurf eines Programmes für die bildnerische Decoration der Façaden des k. k. Museums für Kunst und Alterthum", in: *Die k. k. Hofmuseen in Wien und Gottfried Semper.* Drei Denkschriften Gottfried Sem- per's herausgegeben von seinen Söhnen, Innsbruck, 1892.

Manfred Semper, *Hasenauer und Semper. Eine Erwiderung und Richtigstellung,* Hamburg, 1895.

Die Votivkirche in Wien. Denkschrift des Baucomités, Vienna, 1879.

Heinrich Wagner, *Handbuch der Architektur,* part 4, vol. 6, fascicle 4: Josef Durm, Hermann Ende (eds.) *Gebäude für Sammlungen und Ausstellungen,* 2nd ed., Stuttgart, 1906.

Johann Joachim Winckelmann, *Geschichte der Kunst des Altertums,* Vienna, 1776.

Beat Wyss, "Habsburgs Panorama. Zur Ikonologie und „Psychoanalyse" der Wiener Museumsbauten", in: Gabriele Helke (ed.), *100 Jahre Kunsthistorisches Museum. Das Kunsthistorische Museum als Denkmal und Gesamtkunst- werk* (Jahrbuch der kunsthistorischen Sammlungen in Wien, Vol. 88 [N. S. Vol. 52]), 1992.

Index of Persons